CW00363982

THE
OCEANS

A CELEBRATION

WAVES BREAKING

(Kim Westerskov)

OVERLEAF: A SCHOOL OF FUSILIERS OVER A CHALICE CORAL

(David Hall)

THE
OCEANS

A CELEBRATION

A CORAL GROUPER
(Jeffrey L. Rotman)

COMPILED BY THE LIVING EARTH FOUNDATION

Editor: LISA SILCOCK

Commissioning Editor: DAMIEN LEWIS   Consultant Editor: ROBERT BISSET

Introduction by DAVID BELLAMY

Ebury Press · London

FIRST PUBLISHED 1993

1 3 5 7 9 10 8 6 4 2

COPYRIGHT © LIVING EARTH FOUNDATION 1993

THE LIVING EARTH FOUNDATION HAVE ASSERTED THEIR RIGHT UNDER THE
COPYRIGHT, DESIGNS AND PATENTS ACT, 1988, TO BE IDENTIFIED AS THE AUTHORS
OF THIS WORK.

ALL RIGHTS RESERVED. NO PART OF THIS PUBLICATION MAY BE REPRODUCED,
STORED IN A RETRIEVAL SYSTEM, OR TRANSMITTED IN ANY FORM OR BY ANY
MEANS, ELECTRONIC, MECHANICAL, PHOTOCOPYING, RECORDING OR OTHERWISE,
WITHOUT PRIOR PERMISSION OF THE COPYRIGHT OWNERS.

CO-ORDINATING EDITOR: SUE PHILLPOTT
DESIGNER: DAVID FORDHAM
RESEARCH ASSISTANTS: DEBBIE NIBLOCK, SADIE NICHOLS,
KAREN RADEL AYLWARD
PRODUCTION BY HELEN EVERSON

FIRST PUBLISHED IN THE UNITED KINGDOM IN 1993 BY
EBURY PRESS LIMITED
RANDOM HOUSE, 20 VAUXHALL BRIDGE ROAD, LONDON SW1V 2SA

RANDOM HOUSE AUSTRALIA (PTY) LIMITED
20 ALFRED STREET, MILSONS POINT, SYDNEY
NEW SOUTH WALES 2061, AUSTRALIA

RANDOM HOUSE NEW ZEALAND LIMITED
18 POLAND ROAD, GLENFIELD
AUCKLAND 10, NEW ZEALAND

RANDOM HOUSE SOUTH AFRICA (PTY) LIMITED
PO BOX 337, BERGVLEI, SOUTH AFRICA

RANDOM HOUSE UK LIMITED REG. NO. 954009

A CIP CATALOGUE RECORD FOR THIS BOOK
IS AVAILABLE FROM THE BRITISH LIBRARY

ISBN 0 09 177882 4

TYPESET BY SX COMPOSING LTD, RAYLEIGH, ESSEX

PRINTED IN ITALY BY OFFICINE GRAFICHE DE AGOSTINI, NOVARA

PAPERS USED BY EBURY PRESS ARE NATURAL RECYCLABLE PRODUCTS MADE
FROM WOOD GROWN IN SUSTAINABLE FORESTS.
COLOUR SEPARATIONS BY MAGNACRAFT LTD, LONDON, USING
ENVIRONMENTALLY FRIENDLY INKS.

CONTENTS

INTRODUCTION

PROFESSOR DAVID BELLAMY

SALT WATER COVERS SEVENTY PER CENT OF PLANET EARTH TO AN AVERAGE depth of four thousand metres (13,000 ft). A proportion of this vast volume of liquid escapes as pure vapour into the atmosphere, and some is blown over the land as clouds. Every day, these clouds moisten our otherwise dry islands and continents and replenish our rivers with eighty cubic kilometres (19 cubic miles) of fresh water, shed as rain, sleet or snow. All life depends utterly on water, and this process, which begins and ends in the sea, supplies it to every organism on land: that is, to every plant, to every animal, and to a human population now approaching six billion.

Our intimate relationship with the sea goes back three and a half billion years, when life as we know it began to develop in the oceans. Today, the sea is home to about half of all the species of plants and animals, discounting the insects, that inhabit our planet. From the smallest to the largest, each has a vital part to play in maintaining the balance of life on earth.

Swarms of microscopic algae known as coccolithophores, for example, manufacture protective crystal shells using carbon dioxide. Their skeletons, along with the bodies of other creatures, fall in a constant rain into the abyssal depths. Tiny corals also use carbon dioxide to build their great limestone reefs. Thus these minute creatures lock up great quantities of the most abundant greenhouse gas in the depths of the sea, out of harm's way – and produce oxygen into the bargain.

At the opposite end of the scale, we are at last learning that the great whales and their kin have more to offer us alive than dead. For the present, this is one of conservation's success stories, and most people now abhor the idea of killing these sentient, highly intelligent creatures, whose behaviour offers many parallels with our own: whales 'talk' to each other, make love, live in family groups, teach their children and even sing complex songs. Yet a few 'cultured' and very rich nations want to resume hunting, claiming that whales can be harvested on a scientifically sustainable basis. A harpoon often takes many hours to kill even a small minke whale, while its family looks on in distress.

It is clear that despite hard campaigning by world experts and hundreds of thousands of other intelligent people, the message still has not got through to many of those most responsible for the oceans. As I write this, thousands of birds, otters, seals, fish and other creatures are endangered by the oil leaking from a tanker aground on the Shetland coast. It is, say the authorities, another accident that should not have happened: but what are they doing about preventing the next one, and about marine conservation as a whole?

Time is running out for the oceans. Please read this book, because the extraordinary life that it celebrates is exactly what is at stake. Then join the campaigners and help us to fight for the oceans' survival: for their own sake, for yourselves and for your children's future.

A GREY ANGEL FISH, GRAND BAHAMA
(Richard Herrmann)

7

CHAPTER ONE

BEYOND THE MIRROR SURFACE:
THE OCEAN ECOSYSTEM
DR JULIAN CALDECOTT

It's easy to think of the world's surface in the old way: as a pattern of land, with emptiness in between. Realization can come suddenly, though. Maybe while watching waves explode against a rugged coastline, or when snorkelling or scuba diving; perhaps in the first few seconds after the cold plunge from a dinghy, when you roll over and look down at the other two thirds of Creation. After that, it's all different.

I MAGINE: YOU ARE DEEP IN TRANSPARENT WATER, BESIDE a rocky wall off, say, the coast of Sulawesi, Indonesia. The wall is encrusted with corals, sponges, tentacled anemones, sea-squirts and algae; the seabed is invisibly far below, the mirror surface high above. A spectacular array of swimming creatures glide and dart around you. There is a giant spotted eagle-ray; some blue surgeonfish, and clown triggerfish; a dense pack of several hundred blackfin barracuda; banded sea-snakes; green turtles; gigantic Napoleon wrasse; torrents of small, bright lunar fusiliers; masses of silver jacks and trevallies; even white-tipped reef sharks.

At night, by flashlight, you see different creatures: mantis shrimps, delicately branching gorgonians, feather-stars, spiny lobsters, and parrotfish sleeping in bags of mucus within little caves. There are brittle-stars creeping, sea-stars feeding, and urchins waving their pencil-thick spines. Before, this rock wall was just a darker line in the sea, perhaps glanced at from an aeroplane window. Now, you hesitate to order seafish from a

1 A GARIBALDI, CATALINA ISLAND, CALIFORNIA
(Richard Herrmann)
A SHALLOW-WATER DAMSELFISH WHICH USUALLY INHABITS KELP FORESTS, THE GARIBALDI IS EXTREMELY TERRITORIAL. THE MALE GUARDS THE EGGS, MAKING DEEP GUTTURAL SOUNDS WHEN AGITATED, AND WILL CHARGE POTENTIAL PREDATORS, NO MATTER WHAT THEIR SIZE. FORMERLY THREATENED BY ENTHUSIASTIC COLLECTING FOR AQUARIUMS, THE GARIBALDI IS NOW THE STATE MARINE FISH OF CALIFORNIA, AND IS OFFICIALLY PROTECTED.

restaurant menu; you wonder about how the sea works, and with it, the world.

The ocean waters cover two thirds of our planet's surface, circling the world in unbroken continuity. They are the ballast and buffer of earth's ecology, the birthplace of its plants and animals, and the major store of living resources and chemicals necessary for life. The seas stabilize the atmosphere, and are the source of the weather which affects us on land. They remain, however, largely unknown: much research is still needed to identify their inhabitants and to understand their ecology. Our lack of knowledge is a product not only of the sea's inaccessibility, but also of its fundamental *difference*. For to penetrate the glittering surface of the sea is to enter an alien realm, where entirely new rules of biological diversity and energy flow apply.

From our terrestrial viewpoint, we tend to think of biological diversity in terms of trees and ferns, birds and mammals. But unless you venture beneath the sea you will never encounter almost half of the fundamental kinds of living creature that exist on our planet. Zoology distinguishes thirty-three different animal phyla in the world, each phylum representing a basic life-form design. The oceans are host to thirty-two of these phyla, fifteen of which are *exclusively* marine.

Many oceanic life forms look truly extraordinary to our eyes, accustomed only to creatures adapted to terrestrial living. For example, the floating pink siphonophore looks like a translucent eyeball with a blue iris. It pulsates up and down as it drifts, controlling its buoyancy by secreting carbon monoxide into its float. Behind it trail some 10 metres (over 30 ft) of fine, contractile, stinging tentacles: a deadly trap for prey.

Shapes mislead: the pale, graceful little 'plants' on the coral wall are actually animals – sea-fan hydroids. The multi-tentacled 'worm' foraging over the coral is as much a mollusc as is the garden slug; it has stolen the stinging cells of its prey and incorporated them into its tentacles for its own defence. The pieces of fine white cloth clinging to the sharp edge of the reef are not rags, but animals – membranous ribbon bryozoans.

The apparently bizarre appearance of such life forms is, though, as logical an evolutionary solution to conditions in the sea as the legs of animals are to life on land. For instance, because sea-water supports living tissue, floating or weak-swimming marine organisms do not need the heavy skeletons required to support land plants and animals. Many sea creatures are delicate and jelly-like; jellyfish are familiar examples. Furthermore, the physical structure and lifestyle of every marine organism reflects its place in the ocean. The sea provides a much more three-dimensional environment than the land, with a far greater volume of space available for use by living organisms. This space is extremely varied in the conditions it provides for its inhabitants: light, temperature, salinity, nutrient concentration and pressure all differ greatly with place and time.

In shallow waters, for example, light is plentiful. Here the variety of colour and form is astonishing. Consider the rippling purple and orange blotches of the leopard flatworm; the goofy-mouthed, colour-changing scribbled filefish; or the intricate blue-black-gold *cloisonné* work of the 'male' (actually sex-reversed) spotted boxfish. In these high-visibility waters, such gaudiness is no evolutionary accident. Markings may serve as camouflage; but bright, distinctive patterns are more often visual signals, indicating a poisonous nature to would-be predators, or advertising the species identity, sexual status or social rank of individuals.

Above 100 metres (330 ft) or so, there is enough light to support photosynthesis – the process by which plants convert sunlight and atmospheric gases into organic materials for growth. Here, microscopic free-floating plants called phytoplankton proliferate. These form the base of marine food chains, directly or indirectly supporting every one of the sea's creatures. The energy harnessed by plant plankton is passed on to the many tiny animals which prey on them – the so-called zooplankton, including minute shrimps, sticky-armed ctenophorans, and innumerable marine larvae. Zooplankton are, in turn, the staple diet of filter-feeding creatures – from corals, sponges and tiny fish fry to the enormous whale-shark and the great baleen whales themselves.

Above filter-feeders in the food chain comes an amazing array of secondary consumers. These include multi-species aggregations of brilliantly coloured parrotfish, which can crush corals like biscuits in their fused, beak-like teeth, and the omnivorous Picasso triggerfish – known to Hawaiians as *humuhumu-nukunuku-a-pua'a*: 'the fish which grunts like a pig'. More specialized is the crown-of-thorns starfish, which everts its stomach through its mouth to envelop and digest coral polyps.

Continue up the predator hierarchy, to fish which pounce from the sky at dusk and dawn – like the crocodile needlefish, which has been known to impale fishermen in their boats. Others ambush from cover, or stalk the bottom at night. The sequence ends with top predators which have no need of such subtleties: the killer whale, the great barracuda, and the aptly named requiem sharks. Still other creatures target the dead or the dying, contributing to the dramatic rate with which life in the ocean is recycled. Unconsumed dead plankton and animal carcasses become drifting and sedimenting resources for foragers like heart-urchins, sea cucumbers, shrimps and crabs. The remaining debris drifts downwards five km (3 miles) or more, where it becomes food for a vast number of deep-living species.

Sediment from the remains of ocean life gradually accumulates as a shroud over the seabed, mixing with sand, eventually to settle and harden into layers of rock. Older seabeds, reflecting many millions of years of prehuman history, can be seen when reconstructed from seismic surveys. These provide clues to the dynamic, impermanent nature of the oceans and of the earth itself. Here is the crest of a fossilized coral reef or islet, once overwhelmed by rising sea levels and gradually covered by new layers of rock; there, a gentle dome over the remains of prehistoric vegetation long since buried.

Constantly shifting and undulating, the seabed has altered dramatically over hundreds of millions of years. Continents have moved and whole sections have been swallowed. Huge volcanic mountain ranges, their tips sometimes emerging as islands above the sea, have appeared; elsewhere, the ancient ocean crust has been squeezed back down into the earth's fiery interior. Sea levels rise and fall: just 20,000 years ago, they were 130 metres (430 ft) lower than today, and dry land linked much of the Indonesian archipelago to Asia and Australia.

Dramatic though they are, these are natural changes which have taken place over millions of years, and ecosystems have tended to adapt themselves accordingly. However, there are some changes, brought about by our own species, that they cannot accommodate. Human societies throughout history have differed widely in their willingness to maintain natural systems by using them sustainably, and in their ability to do harm. On the one hand, there are healthy mangroves which have undergone a thousand years' use by fisherfolk and collectors of such products as thatching materials, charcoal, seaweed, palm sugar, honey, fish and shellfish. On the other, there are crippled wildernesses of acidic mud left from a dozen years' clearfelling of mangroves for rayon pulp and disposable chop-sticks. Coastal settlements have often been the springboards of civilization, trade, colonization and conquest. Alien life forms and alien values have been introduced, wreaking ecological witchcraft on the life and very substance of the world's ocean systems.

The ecology, geology, biogeography and sociology of the oceans constitute a vital part of the human and natural history of our planet. The influence of the oceans has been decisive in the past, and will be equally so in the future. It is to the many roles of the oceans that this book is dedicated, as a celebration – with affection, astonishment, respect and hope.

2 ORANGE SEA-PERCH OVER A CORAL REEF, RED SEA

(Linda Pitkin)

THESE FISH, SOMETIMES CALLED 'BASSLETS', ARE COMMON IN THE SHALLOW WATERS ABOVE THE RED SEA REEFS (THIS ONE IS OFF THE COAST OF EGYPT). SMALL NUMBERS OF MAGENTA-COLOURED MALES PRESIDE OVER LARGE HAREMS OF ORANGE FEMALES.

3

3   A BARRACUDA, GRAND CAYMAN, WEST INDIES

(J. Michael Kelly)

BARRACUDA CAN REACH 30 KG (66 LB) OR MORE IN WEIGHT AND ARE FEROCIOUS
PREDATORS, EQUIPPED WITH LARGE JAWS AND RAZOR-SHARP TEETH. THEY HUNT
ALONE OR IN SMALL SCHOOLS, CRUISING AROUND THE REEF EDGE IN SEARCH OF
STRAY FISH, WHICH THEY PURSUE RELENTLESSLY. SOMETIMES THEY WILL ALSO
EAT CARRION. SOME TWENTY SPECIES ARE FOUND WORLDWIDE, MAINLY IN
TROPICAL SEAS. IN SOME WATERS THEY HAVE BEEN KNOWN TO ATTACK
SWIMMERS AND DIVERS, BUT THIS IS PROBABLY A CASE OF MISTAKEN IDENTITY:
THE FLASH OF A WATCH MAY RESEMBLE A DARTING FISH. BARRACUDAS
THEMSELVES ARE OFTEN HUNTED BY HUMANS FOR THEIR MEAT.

4

4   A TARPON AMONGST A SCHOOL OF SILVERSIDES

(J. Michael Kelly)

THOUGH THEY PREFER SHALLOWS AND MANGROVE FLATS, TARPON ARE OFTEN FOUND DRIFTING THROUGH THE CANYONS AND CAVES OF THE CARIBBEAN REEFS AT DEPTHS OF 12-18 METRES (40-60 FT). THEY CAN GROW TO A LENGTH OF 2 METRES (6.5 FT). GOLDFISH-SIZED SILVERSIDES DRIFT THROUGH THE SAME CAVES AND CANYONS IN DENSE SCHOOLS. WHEN NIGHT FALLS, BOTH SPECIES ABANDON THEIR DEEPER DAYTIME HABITATS TO FEED CLOSER TO THE SURFACE, PLUNGING BACK DOWN AGAIN AS DAY BREAKS.

5   A BLUE COD SWALLOWING A WRASSE

(Darryl Torckler/Tony Stone Worldwide)

PREDATORY FISH SUCH AS THE BLUE COD PATROL THE DEEPER WATERS AROUND CORAL REEFS, SEIZING INCAUTIOUS PREY LIKE THIS WRASSE.

6

7

6   A SEA-FAN, CARIBBEAN

(Linda Pitkin)

SEA-FANS ARE COLONIES OF CORALS KNOWN AS GORGONIANS, OR HORNY
CORALS; THEY HAVE A MUCH MORE FLEXIBLE CASING THAN THE REEF-FORMING
STONY VARIETY. PURPLE SEA-FANS ARE ABUNDANT THROUGHOUT THE
CARIBBEAN. THEY TYPICALLY LIVE DEEPER DOWN THE FACE OF THE REEF,
WHERE THE WATER IS COOLER AND THE SUNLIGHT THINNER. GROWING AT RIGHT
ANGLES TO THE PREVAILING CURRENT, FANS STRAIN MICROSCOPIC PARTICLES OF
FOOD FROM THE WATER. THE TENTACLES OF THE POLYPS – THE MULTITUDES OF
TINY UNITS THAT MAKE UP THE FAN – MAKE IT VIRTUALLY IMPOSSIBLE FOR ANY
SMALL DRIFTING ORGANISM TO PASS SAFELY BY.

7   A GORGONIAN, CUBA

(Linda Pitkin)

HORNY CORALS ARE FOUND GROWING ALL OVER REEFS OF STONY CORAL. THEY
MAY BE FAN-SHAPED (6), WHIP-LIKE, BUSHY OR PLUME-LIKE, AS HERE. MORE
FLEXIBLE GORGONIANS SUCH AS THIS ONE CAN WITHSTAND QUITE STRONG
CURRENTS THAT WOULD DESTROY THE MORE BRITTLE, DELICATE SEA-FAN.

8

8   A LONG-NOSE HAWKFISH IN GORGONIAN CORAL, INDO-PACIFIC
(Norbert Wu)
WITH THEIR REMARKABLE PATTERNING, THESE HAWKFISH ARE ADMIRABLY
DISGUISED WITHIN THE RED GORGONIANS' BRANCHES, WHERE THEY ARE
COMMONLY SEEN – THOUGH THEY ARE ALSO FOUND ON BLACK CORAL. THEIR
CAMOUFLAGE NOT ONLY PROTECTS THEM FROM PREDATORS, BUT ALSO ENABLES
THEM TO AMBUSH THEIR PREY – USUALLY SMALL CRUSTACEANS.

9   A PARROTFISH, BORNEO
(Norbert Wu)
THERE ARE MANY SPECIES OF THESE BRILLIANT FISH. THEY LIVE AROUND CORAL
REEFS, AND THE LARGEST GROW TO ONE METRE (OVER 3 FT) OR MORE. MOST ARE
GRAZERS, SCRAPING CORAL FROM THE REEFS AND CRUNCHING IT IN THEIR
SHARP MOUTHPARTS IN ORDER TO EXTRACT THE POLYPS WITHIN IT. THE
PULVERIZED CORAL THAT THEY EXCRETE CONTRIBUTES TO THE SILT AROUND
REEFS. SOME PARROTFISH SLEEP DRAPED IN A MUCUS COVERING, WHICH
PROBABLY HELPS THEM TO AVOID BEING DETECTED BY PREDATORS. LIKE ALL
THE WRASSES, SOME FEMALE PARROTFISH CHANGE SEX, BECOMING BRIGHTLY
PATTERNED MALES.

9

10 A SEA HORSE, SEA OF CORTEZ
(Mark Conlin/Planet Earth)
SEA HORSES INHABIT SHALLOW
COASTAL WATERS AROUND THE
REEFS OF TROPICAL AND WARM
TEMPERATE SEAS. THEY HAVE
PREHENSILE TAILS, WITH WHICH
THEY ANCHOR THEMSELVES TO
SEAWEEDS, CORAL AND SPONGES.
THEIR EYES MOVE INDEPENDENTLY
LIKE THOSE OF CHAMELEONS ON
LAND, PERMITTING THEM TO SCAN
TWO DIRECTIONS AT ONCE, FOR
FOOD AND FOR PREDATORS. SEA
HORSES HAVE NO TEETH, BUT WITH
THEIR ELONGATED SNOUTS THEY
SUCK IN THE SHRIMPS AND
COPEPODS ON WHICH THEY FEED.

10

11 A SLENDER FILEFISH IN GORGONIAN CORAL, BELIZE
(Michael J. Kelly)
THE SLENDER FILEFISH IS FOUND MAINLY IN THE CARIBBEAN. TWO TO 6 CM (1-2 IN) LONG, IT USUALLY LIVES CAMOUFLAGED IN GORGONIANS (AS HERE), POSITIONED VERTICALLY; BUT IT MAY SOMETIMES BE SEEN ON SEAGRASS BEDS, IN ROCKY- OR SANDY-BOTTOMED WATERS. SOME SPECIES OF FILEFISH CAN VARY THEIR COLOUR TO MATCH THEIR SURROUNDINGS. THEIR DIET IS VERY VARIED, AND INCLUDES SPONGES, HYDROIDS AND STINGING CORAL.

11

12

12 A RED IRISH LORD, VANCOUVER ISLAND

(Linda Pitkin)

DESPITE ITS BRIGHT COLOURING, THIS FISH IS WELL DISGUISED IN ITS ROCKY
SEA-FLOOR HABITAT IN THE TEMPERATE WATERS OF NORTH AMERICA'S PACIFIC
COAST. THERE IT LIES, WAITING TO AMBUSH CRUSTACEANS, MOLLUSCS AND
SMALL FISH THAT STRAY TOO NEAR. SINCE IT INHABITS COASTAL WATERS, IT IS
SUSCEPTIBLE TO THE DUMPING OF WASTES AND TO RUN-OFF FROM THE LAND.

13

13   A STARRY PUFFERFISH, SOLOMON ISLANDS

(B. Jones & M. Shimlock)

ALSO KNOWN AS THE WHITE-SPOTTED PUFFER OR STARS-AND-STRIPES PUFFER,
THIS SOLITARY FISH MAY GROW UP TO 50 CM (20 IN). IT IS A POOR SWIMMER, AND
USUALLY RESIDES NEAR THE SEA FLOOR IN SHALLOWISH WATERS. LIKE ALL
PUFFERS, IT INFLATES ITSELF, WHEN ALARMED, BY DRAWING WATER INTO A
POUCH NEAR ITS STOMACH. IT IS FAIRLY COMMON IN THE INDO-PACIFIC, AS FAR
NORTH AS JAPAN.

14 *ACROPORA* CORAL, SOLOMON
ISLANDS

(Norbert Wu)
CORALS OF THE GENUS *ACROPORA*
ADOPT MORE GROWTH FORMS
THAN ANY OTHER, WITH THE SAME
SPECIES BEING FOUND IN
STAGHORN, PLATE, TABULAR AND
BRANCHING SHAPES. VIGOROUS
GROWERS, THEY ARE THE
DOMINANT COLONIZING CORALS
ON MOST REEFS, AND ARE AMONG
THE FIRST TO OCCUPY NEW
HABITATS SUCH AS UNDERSEA LAVA
FLOWS. THEY CAN LIVE ONLY IN
SHALLOW WATER, HOWEVER,
WHERE THE SUNLIGHT IS STRONG
ENOUGH FOR THE SYMBIOTIC
ALGAE (ZOOXANTHELLAE) WHICH
INHABIT CORAL POLYPS TO
PHOTOSYNTHESIZE, THUS
PROVIDING FOOD FOR THE CORAL
ITSELF. TO PREVENT DEHYDRATION
WHEN EXPOSED DURING LOW
TIDES, THE CORAL SECRETES A
PROTECTIVE MUCUS.

15

15   A GIANT GREEN ANEMONE, SAN MIGUEL ISLAND, CALIFORNIA
(Richard Herrmann)
THE CARNIVOROUS ANEMONE'S TENTACLES ARE ARMED WITH STINGING CELLS
THAT ARE LETHAL TO SMALL CREATURES. THE TENTACLES PUSH THE DEAD PREY
INTO THE CENTRAL MOUTH. THE GIANT GREEN IS CONSIDERED THE CLASSIC
PACIFIC ANEMONE. UNLIKE MOST, WHICH LIVE BELOW THE TIDAL ZONE AND ARE
CONTINUALLY UNDER WATER, THESE CAN BE FOUND EXPOSED IN TIDAL POOLS
ALONG THE CALIFORNIAN COAST. AT NIGHT THEY FOLD THEIR TENTACLES INSIDE
THEIR BODIES FOR PROTECTION.

16

16 A TUBE CORAL POLYP, PHILIPPINES

(David Hall)

THOUGH TECHNICALLY ONE OF THE HARD CORALS, TUBE CORALS DO NOT FORM THE CLOSE COLONIES THAT BUILD REEFS, BUT GROW A FEW CENTIMETRES APART FROM EACH OTHER. AT NIGHT, THE POLYPS EMERGE FROM THEIR HARD TUBES AND EXTEND THEIR STINGING TENTACLES TO FEED ON THE MINUTE ORGANISMS DRIFTING BY. AT FULL STRETCH, EACH POLYP MAY BE 5 CM (2 IN) LONG.

17

17 AN ORANGE BALL CORALLIMORPH, GRAND CAYMAN

(J. Michael Kelly)

DESPITE ITS RESEMBLANCE TO THAT FAMILY, THIS IS NOT AN ANEMONE. LIVING IN CORAL CREVICES OR SAND, IT COMES OUT AT NIGHT TO FEED, EXTENDING ITS TRANSLUCENT POLYPS WITH THEIR BALL-LIKE TIPS. IT QUICKLY RETRACTS THEM IF DISTURBED.

18

19

20

18   A SEA-SLUG, *HERMISSENDA CRASSICORNIS*, ON AN ANEMONE

(Richard Herrmann)

SEA-SLUGS, OR NUDIBRANCHS, ARE UNSHELLED MARINE SNAILS. THERE ARE A
LARGE NUMBER OF SPECIES – FOR EXAMPLE, OVER 400 OF THE *CHROMODORIS*
NUDIBRANCHS EXIST IN THE INDIAN AND PACIFIC OCEANS. EACH SPECIES HAS A
DISTINCTIVE BRIGHT COLOURING.

19   A *NEMBROTHA CRISTATA* ON CORAL, BORNEO

(Linda Pitkin)

SEA-SLUGS OCCUR IN TROPICAL OCEANS ALL OVER THE WORLD, IN SHALLOW
WATERS AROUND CORAL REEFS. THIS ONE APPEARS TO FEED ON SEA-SQUIRTS,
AND PRODUCES A TOXIN WHICH MAKES IT REPUGNANT TO MOST PREDATORS. ITS
VIVID COLORATION MAY SERVE TO WARN OF ITS POISONOUS NATURE.

20   A SPANISH SHAWL SEA-SLUG

(Norbert Wu)

AS WELL AS SEA-SQUIRTS, SEA-SLUGS FEED MAINLY ON ANEMONES, SPONGES AND
HORNY CORALS. OFTEN THEIR FOOD IS TOXIC, AND MANY SEA-SLUGS
INCORPORATE THE TOXINS FROM THEIR PREY INTO THEIR OWN TENTACLE-LIKE
FEATHERY OUTGROWTHS – WHICH FUNCTION LIKE GILLS – AND USE THEM FOR
DEFENCE. ALTERNATIVELY, TOXINS ARE SOMETIMES STORED IN WHITISH BUMPS
ON THE ANIMALS' SKIN. MOST SEA-SLUGS ARE SMALL, BUT ON AUSTRALIA'S
BARRIER REEF ONE SPECIES REACHES 30 CM (12 IN).

21

21 A SEA-SLUG EGG RIBBON, SOLOMON ISLANDS

(B. Jones & M. Shimlock)

THE SPAWNING MASS OF THE SPANISH DANCER SEA-SLUG, FOUND THROUGHOUT
THE INDO-PACIFIC REGION. SEA-SLUGS LAY EGG RIBBONS OF THE SAME COLOUR
AS THEIR OWN DOMINANT COLOUR, USUALLY SPIRALLED AROUND THEIR
FAVOURITE FOOD. SOME MASSES CAN CONTAIN A MILLION EGGS.

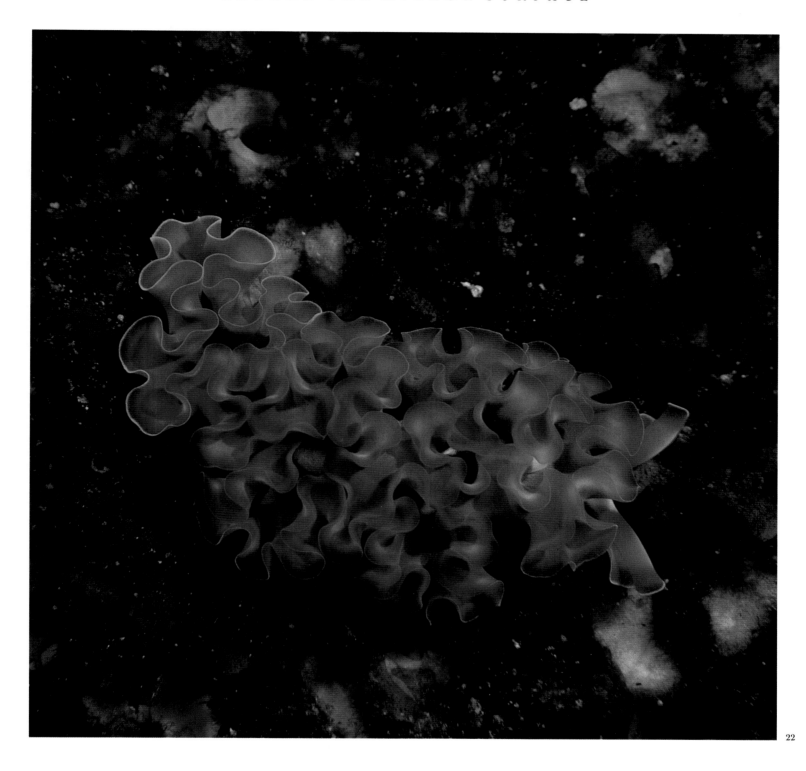

22

22   A LETTUCE SEA-SLUG, GRAND CAYMAN

(J. Michael Kelly)

THE NUMEROUS RUFFLES ON ITS BACK HAVE EARNED THIS NUDIBRANCH THE
NAME OF 'LETTUCE SEA-SLUG'. COMMON IN THE CARIBBEAN, FLORIDA AND THE
BAHAMAS, THE SPECIES SPORTS VARIOUS SHADES OF GREEN AND THE
OCCASIONAL BLUE, AND SOMETIMES HAS YELLOW OR RED MARKINGS.

23

24

25

23   A SLATE PENCIL URCHIN, HAWAII
(Norbert Wu)
THIS RARE SEA URCHIN IS EQUIPPED WITH THICK, STRONG, HOLLOW SPINES
WHICH GROW UP TO 13 CM (5 IN) LONG AND ARE VALUED AS BEADS.

24   A RADIANT STAR URCHIN, PAPUA NEW GUINEA
(David Hall)
ANOTHER OF THE LESS COMMON URCHINS, THE RADIANT STAR LIVES IN
SHALLOW WATER AMONGST SEAGRASS BEDS, WHERE IT SUSTAINS ITSELF ON
DEBRIS. UP TO 20 CM (8 IN) ACROSS, IT HAS HIGHLY VENOMOUS SPINES.

25   A FIRE SEA URCHIN, PHILIPPINES
(Norbert Wu)
THE BRILLIANT COLOURS OF THE FIRE SEA URCHIN INDICATE ITS POISONOUS
NATURE. MOST SPECIES OF SEA URCHIN HAVE BOTH LONG AND SHORT SPINES,
AMONG WHICH ARE TO BE FOUND THE LONG, SLENDER TUBE FEET. THE SPINES
ARE MOVABLE, AND AS WELL AS BEING USED FOR PROTECTION, THEY MAY ALSO
SERVE AS LEVERS, HELPING THE TUBE FEET IN LOCOMOTION. A FEW LONG-
SPINED TROPICAL KINDS WALK NOT ON TUBE FEET AT ALL, BUT ON THE TIPS OF
THEIR SPINES. AND SOME URCHINS USE THEIR SPINES, ALONG WITH THEIR TEETH,
TO BURROW INTO HARD ROCK.

CHAPTER TWO

THE BEAUTIFUL AND THE BIZARRE: AN UNPARALLELED DIVERSITY
Dr Tundi Agardy

The oceans cover two thirds of our planet's surface. In terms of sheer volume, they provide a greater range of living conditions than any other environment. Furthermore, life began to evolve in the seas many millions of years before any creature ventured on to dry land. Thus the scene was set for life to develop in the oceans in immense and extraordinary variety: creatures magnificent and monstrous, beautiful and bizarre.

HIGH NOON ON THE HIGH SEAS. FIVE HUNDRED KILOmetres (about 300 miles) from the nearest landmass, the jagged ocean surface suggests unbounded energy, unending motion. Standing waves, translucent grey-green walls of water, are internally propelled towards some distant shore. Over 500 million cubic km (120,000,000 cubic miles) of water are contained in the earth's seas, every molecule moving. There is something undeniably awe-inspiring about this vast, dynamic environment – something which perhaps reminds us, in a primitive, unquantifiable way, of our own evolutionary debt to the sea.

It is a debt shared by all of earth's creatures. Three and a half billion years ago, the primordial oceans spawned the first living organisms, and primitive marine creatures such as sponges, corals and jellyfish flourished for hundreds of millions of years before the invertebrates appeared and began their conquest of dry land. The sea has been the site of experiments in nature for far longer than any other environment, and this has helped to produce an extraordinary variety of marine life: a biological

---

26   BLUE MAOMAO, WITH A STARFISH AND SEA URCHINS
(Kim Westerskov)
THE SEA CONTAINS MANY BASIC LIFE FORMS FOUND NOWHERE ELSE. ONE SUCH IS A VAST GROUP CALLED ECHINODERMS, A PHYLUM OF GREAT AGE AND WORLDWIDE DISTRIBUTION, WHICH INCLUDES SEA URCHINS, STARFISH, BRITTLE-STARS AND SEA CUCUMBERS. THEY HAVE NO HEAD OR TAIL, BUT SHARE A FUNDAMENTAL SYMMETRY.

diversity which is without parallel on land. Whereas only one of the world's thirty-three basic animal life forms, or phyla, is exclusively terrestrial, fifteen are found only in the sea. Consider that phyla subdivide into classes, and thence to orders, families and genera before dividing into species – and you have some indication of the enormous range of life which exists in the ocean realms.

Why is the sea so hospitable to life? As land-living, air-breathing creatures we find it hard to comprehend. But sea-water is perhaps the best living medium there is, holding in readily available liquid solution the resources and chemicals which make life possible. Its heat-storing properties make it a buffer against the variable climate above, and its buoyancy has allowed unconventional physical forms to evolve, heedless of the constraints imposed by gravity.

Paradoxically, though, the marine environment also presents many obstacles to survival. The vastness of the ocean and the sheer power of its movements make it hard for any living thing to be in the right place at the right time. In a constantly changing world, chance plays a big role in survival. Moreover, from surface to seabed, from coast to open ocean, from pole through equator to pole, the sea encompasses an enormous range of environments with endless permutations of light, temperature, movement and availability of nutrients.

Consider, for example, the different set of living conditions present at each layer of the ocean. Near the surface, where upper ocean currents meander towards one another, collide, and veer off again, a thin stretch of sargassum and other weeds collects in a convergence zone. If we look carefully among the floating weed, a bustling and gloriously diverse little community is exposed. Minute copepods and other crustaceans, small fishes, carnivorous comb-jellies, jellyfish, the larvae and fry of coastal fish, even tiny hatchling sea turtles make the rich weed belt their home. Some are temporary visitors, using the weed lines as a nursery, while others stay for their entire lives.

Sunlight penetrates the top hundred metres (330 ft) of the sea, which is called the photic zone. Here, the microscopic algae collectively known as phytoplankton provide the basis for a huge, hungry food chain. Phytoplankton are food, in turn, for zooplankton – small creatures which also live in the photic zone, drifting with the upper currents. These plant and animal plankton are the staple diet of filter-feeding fish and mammals, including the blue whale – the largest mammal on earth.

Travelling down from the surface, we encounter blooms of single-celled and yellow-brown algae; flat, oval crustaceans known as isopods; more tiny free-living copepods, including shrimp-like crustaceans; moon-jellies, and more jellyfish. Here, too, synchronized schools of hunting fish – mackerel, bonito, or young albacore – sweep like silent amorphous ghosts in and out of view. Occasionally, a lone predatory white marlin or mako shark follows in their wake.

Some light even penetrates below the photic zone, to 200-metre (660-ft) depths, casting thick shafts of sunshine which give the water a sacred, ethereal look. But even further down, where the light shafts end in sword-like points and the water turns an ominous blue-black, midwater fishes swim and rest, swim and rest. Some of these species migrate towards the surface to feed during the safety of night, plunging back downwards at the first signs of daylight. Eels journeying from distant river mouths pass by, on their way to the mid-ocean spawning grounds where they will reproduce and then die. Giant shadows are cast when a hunting sperm whale dives into the depths, scattering fish in its wake. Hidden by the darkness, a giant squid flees, propelling itself further downwards.

Below three km (about 2 miles), the so-called abyssal depths are still teeming with thousands of species, each adapted in various ways to the rigours of living without light. Bizarre-looking flashlight fish blink signals to each other through the ink-dark water. An eerie glowing thunderhead formation in the distance reveals itself as a dense congregation of jellyfish, each emitting the cold light known as bioluminescence. Torpedo-shaped leatherback sea turtles that can weigh a thousand kg (2,200 lb) search the depths for such jellyfish, on which they feed.

Even five km (3 miles) down on the pockmarked seabed, life is on the move. Deep-sea creatures, able to survive in darkness and cold, and under immense pressure, await nourishment in the form of dead things drifting down from above. Fish, clams, worms and starfish have been found at up to ten-km (6-mile) depths on the ocean floor.

The ocean thus encourages life in a general sense, but each part of the environment challenges survival in innumerable specific ways. Besides the different levels of the ocean, there are many species-rich coastal habitats – mangroves and mudflats, rocky temperate coastlines, kelp forests, seagrass meadows, and of course coral reefs. Like all marine systems, each supports a highly specialized community of plants and animals, uniquely evolved to deal with the problems of that particular habitat. It is this range of living conditions in the context of a generally welcoming environment that sets the stage for biological diversity. As life forms evolve to become increasingly successful at dealing with ever more precise conditions, new species emerge – leading to the profusion of highly specialized marine forms we know today.

Time, too, is a factor. At work in the seas for three and a half billion years, evolution has produced some extraordinary creatures: jawless fishes, scorpion-like eurypterids, carrion-feeding cone-shelled nautiloids, enormous marine reptiles and giant squid. Some of the strangest variations are now extinct, but many species alive today have been present in the oceans for hundreds of millions of years – and many will probably survive for hundreds of millions more.

The true extent of marine diversity continues to elude us, however. Even close to shore, in waters that we mistakenly believe to be well studied and familiar, mysteries abound. As to the wider seas, and particularly their deepest levels, we know precious little of what is out there. Estimates of the total number of species of ocean fish, for example, range from 15,000 to over 40,000, with the figure of 25,000 most often cited. Confusion arises because some species have not yet been named, and others are named more than once because they vary so much from region to region, male to female. It is thought that up to a million undescribed species exist on the deep sea floor alone, to say nothing of the sombre intricacies of north Pacific kelp beds, which are the most productive of known habitats.

There are even unknown creatures among the rainbow denizens of the much loved, much studied coral reefs – but these may disappear before they have even been identified. Coral reefs are delicate, highly specialized systems, extremely sensitive to environmental change and disturbance. Tourist activities such as diving, fishing and glass-bottomed boating are taking their toll on reefs the world over. The effects of these pursuits are being exacerbated by more general problems such as pollution and increasing temperatures, which are acting to reduce genetic and species diversity before our very eyes.

It is perhaps tempting to compartmentalize the seas, to rank one area over another because it has more species, more unique features, or is simply more appealing. We sometimes speak of marine systems such as coral reefs or mangrove forests as though they were the separate rooms of a living museum: static, immutable and self-sufficient. We are wrong to do so.

The great web of life is nowhere so strongly unified as in the oceans: all habitats, and their communities, are ultimately linked. Changes occurring in one corner of the marine realm make far-reaching ripples. As we survey the unfathomable and mysterious ocean from our comfortable shores, we would do well to remember that we terrestrial beings are also influenced and nourished by the sea in ways that we are only just beginning to understand.

---

27 A BLUE SHARK WITH MACKEREL, UNDER DRIFTING KELP, CALIFORNIA
(Richard Herrmann)
AN OPEN-OCEAN PREDATOR, THE BLUE SHARK WILL DEVOUR ALMOST ANYTHING – INCLUDING MACKEREL. IT IS THE MOST ABUNDANT OF THE 350 KNOWN SHARK SPECIES, AND CAN BE FOUND IN ALL THE WORLD'S OCEANS. LARGE NUMBERS ARE OFTEN SEEN TOGETHER. ITS DOMINANCE MAY BE DUE TO ITS FLEXIBLE EATING HABITS AND NUMEROUS OFFSPRING: FEMALES MAY PRODUCE UP TO 130 YOUNG, WHICH IS FAR MORE THAN USUAL FOR SHARKS.

28 FAIRY BASSLETS AND PULLERS OVER A CORAL REEF, INDONESIA
(Linda Pitkin)
BASSLETS AND PULLERS ARE AMONGST THE MOST COMMON OF CORAL REEF
FISH. THEY TRAVEL IN LARGE SCHOOLS, STAYING CLOSE TO THE SAFETY OF
THE REEF AND FEEDING ON PLANKTON. AT NIGHT THEY RETREAT DEEP INTO
THE CORAL TO SLEEP. WHEN THEY SENSE DANGER, THE WHOLE SCHOOL
DARTS FOR COVER IN UNISON.

29

29 A SPINY BALLOONFISH, GRAND CAYMAN

(J. Michael Kelly)

ONE OF THE PUFFERFISH FAMILY, THE SPINY BALLOONFISH SWIMS SLOWLY NEAR
THE BOTTOM OF SEAGRASS MEADOWS, MANGROVE POOLS AND REEFS, WHERE ITS
COLOURING BLENDS WITH THE SURROUNDINGS. THESE FISH ARE OCCASIONALLY
ENCOUNTERED IN SMALL SCHOOLS. THE DISTINCTIVE LONG SPINES ARE USUALLY
LOWERED, BUT MAY BECOME ERECT EVEN WHEN THE BALLOONFISH IS NOT
INFLATED. AS A DEFENCE WHEN THREATENED, PUFFERFISH INGEST WATER AND
SWELL TO TWICE THEIR SIZE, TO GIVE A MORE FRIGHTENING APPEARANCE. IN
ADDITION, THEY STORE A DEADLY POISON, TETRAODOTOXIN, IN THEIR GONADS
AND LIVER. PREDATORS ARE FEW. SOME SPECIES ADVERTISE THEIR
VENOMOUSNESS WITH BRILLIANT WARNING COLOURS. IN JAPAN PUFFERFISH IS A
DELICACY, BUT EVEN A TRACE OF POISON CAN KILL; SEVERAL PEOPLE DIE EVERY
YEAR AS A RESULT.

30

31

30 A GUINEAFOWL PUFFERFISH, HAWAII

(Norbert Wu)

PUFFERFISH HAVE STRONG, BEAK-LIKE MOUTHS AND FEED ON HARD-SHELLED ANIMALS SUCH AS SEA-URCHINS, MOLLUSCS AND CRABS; SMALL AMOUNTS OF SEAWEED ARE ALSO FOUND IN THEIR STOMACHS.

31 A WOLF EEL, CALIFORNIA

(Norbert Wu)

BOTH ITS FEARSOME APPEARANCE AND ITS NAME BELIE THE SHY NATURE OF THE GIANT WOLF EEL, WHICH MAY GROW TO OVER 2 METRES (6.5 FT) LONG. MALES AND FEMALES FORM LIFELONG PAIRS AND LIVE IN A SINGLE DEN. THE WOLF EEL IS ONE OF THE FEW CREATURES EQUIPPED TO EAT SPINY SEA-URCHINS: IT HAS POWERFUL JAWS, A STRONG SET OF CANINE TEETH TO THE FRONT AND A DOUBLE SET OF MOLARS AT THE BACK.

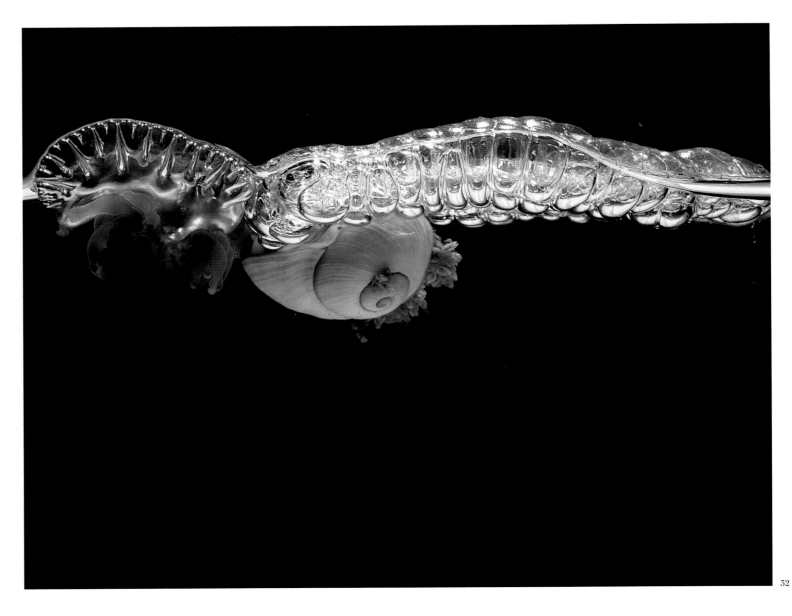

32

33

34

32 and 34   A SEA-SNAIL EATING A PORTUGUESE MAN-O'-WAR
(David Maitland/Planet Earth), **AND ANOTHER FEEDING ON A BY-THE-WIND SAILOR**
(David Maitland/Planet Earth)
THIS SURFACE-DWELLING SNAIL, MEASURING ABOUT A CENTIMETRE (.4 IN)
ACROSS ITS SHELL, SUSPENDS ITSELF UPSIDE DOWN FROM THE SEA'S SURFACE BY
CREATING A FLOATING RAFT OF BUBBLES WITH ITS FOOT.

33   A *GLAUCUS* SEA-SLUG DEVOURING A BY-THE-WIND SAILOR, ATLANTIC
(Peter Parks/Norbert Wu Photography)
AT THE SURFACE OF TROPICAL AND SUB-TROPICAL OPEN OCEAN DWELLS A
COMMUNITY OF ANIMALS CALLED THE 'PLEUSTON', OR 'BLUE COMMUNITY'
(BECAUSE OF ITS PREDOMINANTLY BLUE-MAUVE COLOURING). THE SEA-SLUG
SHOWN HERE HAS A BELLY FULL OF SWALLOWED AIR, WHICH CAUSES IT TO
FLOAT UPSIDE DOWN. THIS SEA-SLUG SPECIES HABITUALLY EATS THE STINGING
TENTACLES OF THE PORTUGUESE MAN-O'-WAR, AND INCORPORATES THE
STINGING TOXINS INTO ITS 'WINGS' FOR ITS OWN DEFENCE. HERE IT IS EATING A
BY-THE-WIND SAILOR, OR *VELELLA*, ANOTHER SURFACE DWELLER, WHOSE FLOAT
IS FULL OF CARBON MONOXIDE.

35

35   A JELLYFISH WITH A PACIFIC BUTTERFLY FISH, CALIFORNIA

(Richard Herrmann)

THE STINGING TENTACLES OF JELLYFISH ARE LETHAL TO MOST FISH, BUT
CERTAIN SPECIES HAVE EVOLVED PARTNERSHIPS WITH PARTICULAR JELLYFISH,
ENABLING THEM TO LIVE UNHARMED AMONG THE TENTACLES. THE PACIFIC
BUTTERFLY FISH, THE COMMENSAL PARTNER OF THIS *PELAGIA COLORATA*
JELLYFISH, GAINS PROTECTION FROM THE TENTACLES, BUT THE JELLYFISH DOES
NOT BENEFIT FROM THE RELATIONSHIP.

36

36 A PEDERSON CLEANER SHRIMP ON A NASSAU GROUPER, GRAND CAYMAN
(J. Michael Kelly)
SOME SHRIMPS FEED ON FISH MUCUS, REMOVING PARASITES AND BACTERIA
FROM THE FISH IN THE PROCESS. THIS 'CLEANER' SHRIMP IS COMMON
THROUGHOUT THE CARIBBEAN, WHERE IT LIVES IN ANEMONES. IN ORDER TO
ATTRACT FISH TO ITS 'CLEANING STATION', IT SITS ON THE ANEMONE, SWAYING
AND WAVING ITS ANTENNAE. FROM ITS PERCH, THE SHRIMP WILL 'SERVICE' A
SUCCESSION OF DIFFERENT FISH, NIBBLING OVER THEIR BODIES IN TURN – IT
WILL EVEN, IF APPROACHED SLOWLY, ATTEMPT TO CLEAN A DIVER'S FINGERS.
THIS ONE, SO TRANSPARENT THAT IT IS BARELY VISIBLE, IS CLEANING THE
GROUPER'S EYE.

37 A *PHYSOPHORA HYDROSTATICA*, SARGASSO SEA

(Heather Angel)
SIPHONOPHORES, WHICH INCLUDE THE PORTUGUESE MAN-O'-WAR, MAKE USE OF THEIR GAS-FILLED FLOATS TO CONTROL THEIR BUOYANCY. THIS ONE PROPELS ITSELF ALONG BY PULSING AND SQUIRTING WATER THROUGH ITS BELL-LIKE STRUCTURES. AN ACTIVE CARNIVORE, IT DETECTS PREY CHEMICALLY AND BY VIBRATIONS, THEN ATTACKS WITH ITS TENTACLES.

37

38   A LION'S MANE JELLYFISH, NEW ZEALAND

(David Hall)

THE WORLD'S LARGEST JELLYFISH, NAMED FOR ITS MASS OF 800 OR SO STINGING TENTACLES AND ITS TAWNY BELL. IN POLAR WATERS IT MAY REACH A METRE (OVER 3 FT) ACROSS, WITH FINGER-THICK TENTACLES TRAILING 10 METRES (33 FT) BEHIND IT. IT IS SAID TO FEEL OUT UNWARY DIVERS AS POTENTIAL PREY. SURPRISINGLY, WHITING LARVAE LIVE SAFELY AMONG THE TENTACLES, GAINING PROTECTION FROM PREDATORS.

38

39   AN OCTOPUS
(Norbert Wu)
THESE SHELL-LESS MOLLUSCS ARE
MAINLY BOTTOM-DWELLERS, IN
WARM TO TEMPERATE WATERS.
THEY LIVE SOLITARY LIVES AMONG
ROCKS OR IN HOLES. THEIR BAG-
LIKE BODIES CONCEAL A SHARP
BEAK, AND THEIR EIGHT MUSCULAR
ARMS ARE EQUIPPED WITH ROWS
OF SUCKERS. THEY LOCATE THEIR
PREY – CRUSTACEANS OR
PLANKTON – WITH THEIR VERY
SHARP EYES. OCTOPUSES CAN
BLEND WITH ALMOST ANY
BACKGROUND: SMALL BAGS OF
PIGMENT IN THEIR SKINS CAN
CONTRACT TO MAKE THE ANIMAL
ALMOST WHITE, OR EXPAND TO
MAKE IT DARK. IN THE GIANT
OCTOPUS THE USUAL DULL
COLOURING CAN CHANGE TO A
ROSY HUE, AS HERE.

39

40

41

40   A CARIBBEAN REEF SQUID AT NIGHT
(J. Michael Kelly)
THE ONLY SQUID COMMON OVER CARIBBEAN REEFS. SQUID SWIM QUICKLY IN LARGE SCHOOLS, BY JET PROPULSION. THEY HAVE A WELL DEVELOPED SENSORY SYSTEM AND EXCEPTIONALLY GOOD EYE-TO-ARM COORDINATION. THE UNDERSIDES OF THE SQUID'S ARMS ARE COVERED WITH SUCTION DISCS; WITH THE TWO MUCH LONGER ARMS IT CAPTURES CRUSTACEANS AND FISH, WHICH IT TEARS APART WITH BEAKY JAWS.

41   A VENOMOUS SEA-SNAKE, PHILIPPINES
(David Hall)
FOUND AMONG CORAL REEFS IN THE INDO-PACIFIC AND IN OTHER ISOLATED AREAS, THIS SEA-SNAKE IS EXTREMELY POISONOUS, ITS VENOM CLOSELY RESEMBLING THAT OF ITS DISTANT RELATIVE THE COBRA. THE FAMILY TO WHICH IT BELONGS CONTAINS THE ONLY REPTILES TO BEAR LIVE YOUNG RATHER THAN LAYING EGGS. IT IS ALSO THE ONLY EXCLUSIVELY MARINE REPTILE, NOT EVEN VISITING LAND TO MATE OR GIVE BIRTH. NONETHELESS IT MUST BREATHE AIR, REMAINING SUBMERGED FOR NO MORE THAN 15 MINUTES AT A TIME.

42

42 A SAWFISH

(Norbert Wu)

LIKE SHARKS, SKATES AND RAYS, THE SAWFISH IS CARTILAGINOUS RATHER THAN
BONY. IT IS POSSIBLE THAT IT USES ITS SERRATED 'BEAK' FOR STUNNING OTHER
FISH AND HACKING THEM APART FOR EATING. THERE ARE 425 SPECIES OF SKATES,
RAYS AND SAWFISH.

43

43   A MANTA RAY, PHILIPPINES
(J. Michael Kelly)
THE GIANT MANTA RAY MAY WEIGH UP TO 2 TONNES, BUT IS HARMLESS DESPITE
ITS AWESOME APPEARANCE. THESE FISH ARE FOUND IN ALL THE WARM OCEANS
OF THE WORLD. UNLIKE MOST RAYS, MANTAS CRUISE NEAR THE SURFACE OF THE
OPEN SEA FEEDING ON PLANKTON, AND ARE SELDOM SEEN OVER REEFS. FROM
TIME TO TIME THEY LEAP CLEAR OF THE WATER, THEN COME CRASHING DOWN
AGAIN – THE REASON FOR THIS PERFORMANCE IS A MYSTERY, BUT IT MAY HELP
TO REMOVE IRRITATING PARASITES, OR IT MAY BE AN EXPRESSION OF THE
ANIMAL'S TERRITORIAL RIGHTS.

44

44   A MANATEE WITH YOUNG, FLORIDA

(Armin Maywald)

THESE SLOW-MOVING CREATURES INCLUDE SEVERAL SPECIES WHICH OCCUR IN
THE ESTUARIES AND COASTAL WATERS OF THE CARIBBEAN AND PARTS OF WEST
AFRICA. THE ONLY EXCLUSIVELY VEGETARIAN MARINE MAMMALS, THEY LIVE ON
VARIOUS SEAWEEDS, NEEDING ABOUT 90 KG (200 LB) A DAY IN ORDER TO
MAINTAIN BODY WEIGHT – WHICH MAY BE 800 KG (1,760 LB). MANATEES ARE
USUALLY 2.5 TO 4.5 METRES (8-15 FT) LONG. THEIR SLUGGISHNESS, POOR SIGHT
AND SENSE OF SMELL MAKE THEM VERY VULNERABLE. THEY ARE ALSO UNDER
THREAT FROM POLLUTION, DESTRUCTION OF HABITAT AND DAMAGE BY
OUTBOARD MOTORS AND FISHING NETS, THOUGH IN SOME AREAS THEY ARE NOW
PROTECTED.

45   GREEN TURTLES MATING, KALIMANTAN, INDONESIA

(B. Jones & M. Shimlock)

GREEN TURTLES ARE FOUND IN MOST TEMPERATE OCEANS, AND FEED ON SEA-
GRASS AND ALGAE. THESE TWO WEIGH 75-100 KG (165-220 LB). MATING TAKES PLACE
THOUSANDS OF MILES AWAY FROM THE TURTLES' FEEDING GROUNDS. WHEN THE
FEMALE DEPOSITS HER HUNDRED OR SO SOFT WHITE EGGS, IT WILL BE ON THE
VERY BEACH WHERE SHE HERSELF HATCHED. LIKE ALL MARINE TURTLE SPECIES,
GREENS ARE ENDANGERED – HUNTING BY HUMANS, THE COLLECTING OF THEIR
EGGS, AND 'DEVELOPMENT' OF THEIR HATCHING BEACHES ARE THEIR GREATEST
HAZARDS.

45

46   A HAMMERHEAD SHARK, GALAPAGOS ISLANDS

(Paul Humann/Jeff Rotman Photography)
THE COMMON HAMMERHEAD
GROWS TO A LENGTH OF 4 METRES
(13 FT) OR MORE. THE T-SHAPED
HEAD, WHICH HAS AN EYE AND A
NOSTRIL AT EACH END OF THE T,
SWINGS FROM SIDE TO SIDE AS THE
SHARK HUNTS – FOR OTHER
SHARKS, RAYS AND SKATES. THEY
ARE SOMETIMES FISHED FOR THEIR
SKIN AND OIL.

46

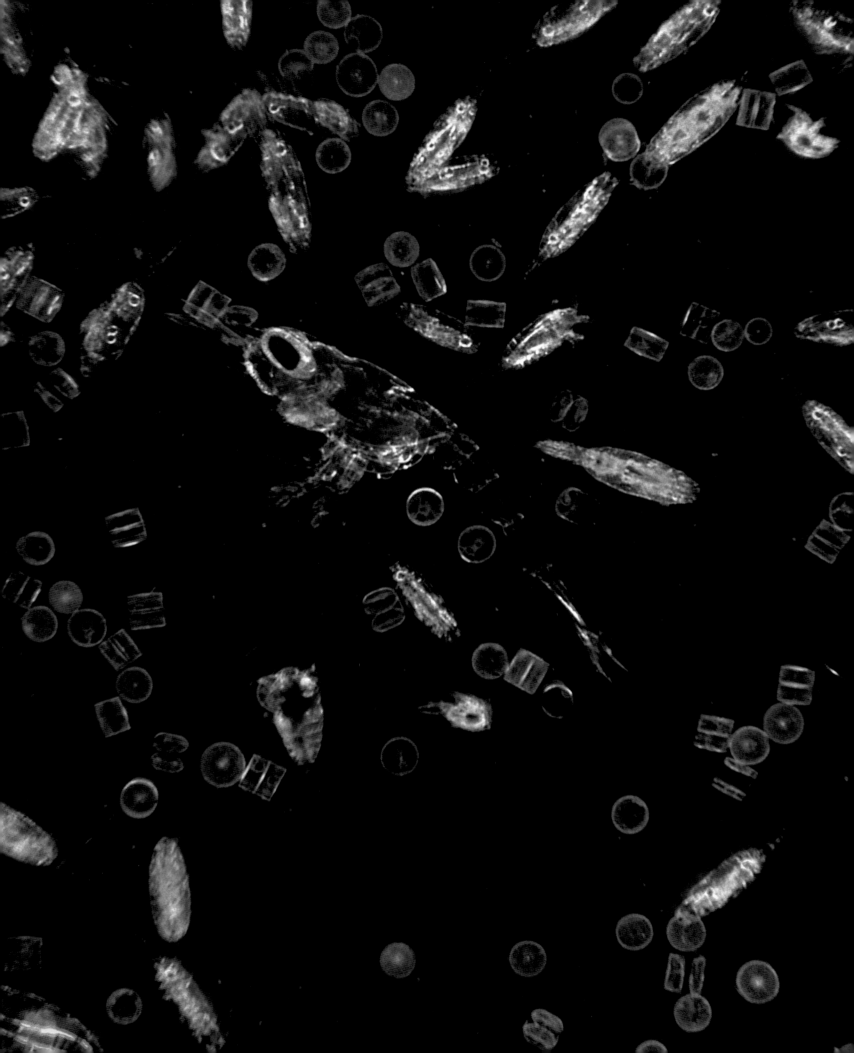

49

49   THE GRASS OF THE OCEANS
(Harold Taylor/OSF)
PHYTOPLANKTON, LIKE GRASS ON LAND, ARE THE PRIMARY PRODUCERS OF THE
OCEAN. THEIR TINY CELLS CONTAIN CHLOROPHYLL, THE GREEN PIGMENT WHICH
ENABLES ALL PLANTS TO PHOTOSYNTHESIZE BY TRAPPING THE ENERGY OF
SUNLIGHT, TO FORM BIOMASS FROM CARBON DIOXIDE AND WATER.

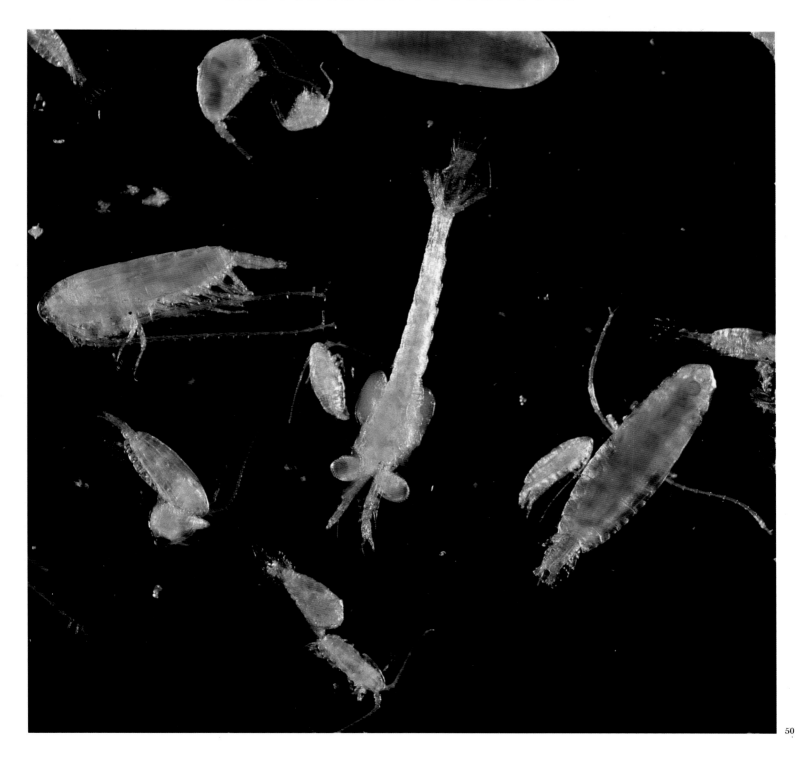

50

50   ASSORTED ANIMAL PLANKTON
(Harold Taylor/OSF)
'ZOOPLANKTON' IS A TERM THAT ENCOMPASSES ALL THE TINY ANIMALS THAT
FEED ON PHYTOPLANKTON, AND ON OTHER ANIMAL PLANKTON. THEY ARE
FOUND AT ALL DEPTHS, BUT ARE MORE NUMEROUS AT THE SURFACE, ESPECIALLY
AT NIGHT. MANY ARE LARVAL FORMS OF CRUSTACEANS, AND WILL EVOLVE INTO
VERY DIFFERENT-LOOKING CREATURES.

51

52

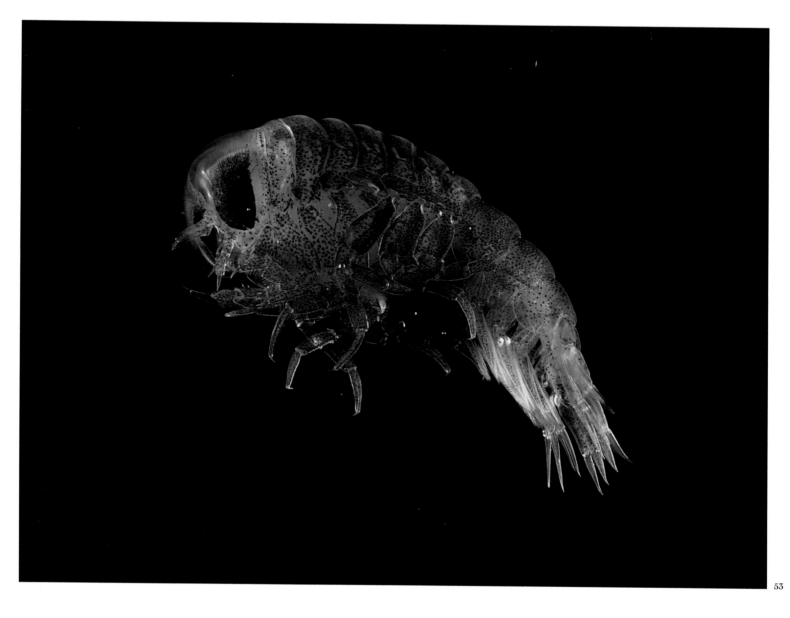

53

51 ATLANTIC KRILL

(Heather Angel)

KRILL ARE ONE OF THE MOST ABUNDANT KINDS OF ANIMAL PLANKTON, PRESENT
THROUGHOUT THE WORLD'S OCEANS. DURING THE POLAR SUMMER, ANTARCTIC
SPECIES GATHER IN MASSIVE SWARMS, TO BE FED ON BY SOME OF THE LARGEST
MARINE CREATURES, INCLUDING BALEEN (FILTER-FEEDING) WHALES, AND
PENGUINS.

52 AN AMPHIPOD, *THEMISTO COMPRESSA*

(Heather Angel)

FOUND IN THE NORTH ATLANTIC, THIS TINY CRUSTACEAN – ANOTHER KIND OF
ZOOPLANKTON – IS NORMALLY A VORACIOUS CARNIVORE, BUT DURING THE
SPRING IT ALSO FEEDS ON PLANT PLANKTON. THERE ARE ABOUT 3,600 SPECIES –
FRESH-WATER AS WELL AS MARINE. AMPHIPODS ARE PARTICULARLY EFFICIENT
SCAVENGERS.

53 A SHALLOW WATER HOPPER

(IOS)

A PREDATOR OF OTHER ANIMAL PLANKTON, THE WATER HOPPER IS ANOTHER
CRUSTACEAN, LIVING AT THE OCEAN'S SURFACE. MOST PLANKTONIC ORGANISMS
HAVE LITTLE OR NO POWER OF LOCOMOTION, AND MERELY DRIFT OR FLOAT,
WHEREVER TIDE OR CURRENT TAKES THEM.

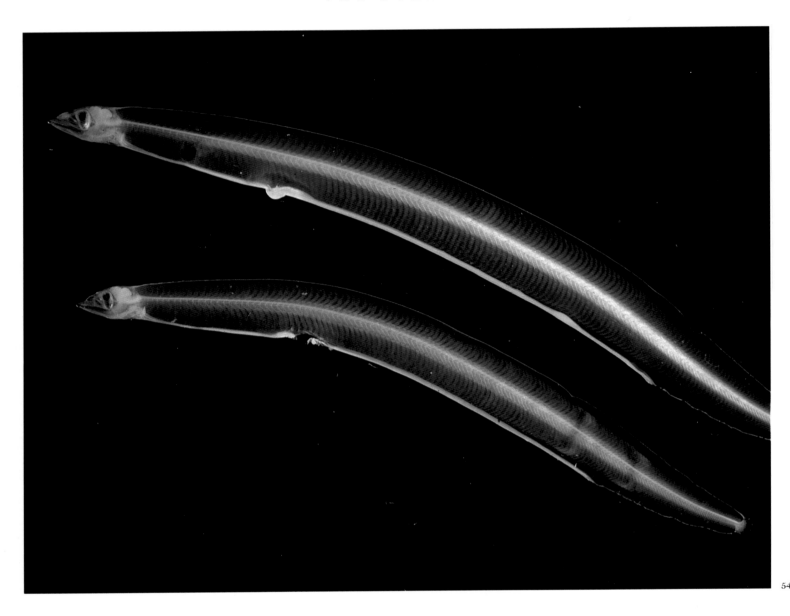

54

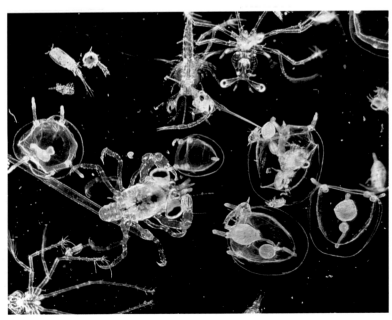

54 and 55   DEEP-SEA EEL LARVAE
(Heather Angel) **AND OTHER ANIMAL**
PLANKTON, BERMUDA
(Peter Parks/OSF)
LIKE MANY MARINE CREATURES,
EELS BEGIN THEIR LIVES AS
PLANKTONIC LARVAE, DRIFTING
WITH THE UPPER CURRENTS. THEIR
EXTREME TRANSPARENCY HELPS
TO CAMOUFLAGE THEM AGAINST
PREDATORS. ANIMAL PLANKTON
INCLUDE A VERY WIDE VARIETY OF
ORGANISMS – IN FACT, EVERY
ANIMAL PHYLUM IS REPRESENTED,
EVEN IF, AS WITH EEL LARVAE,
LIVING AS PLANKTON IS ONLY ONE
PHASE OF THEIR EXISTENCE.
ABOUT 70 PER CENT OF PLANKTON
ARE CRUSTACEANS, OF WHICH THE
PREDOMINANT CLASS IS THE
COPEPODS. IN ADDITION TO
COPEPODS, THE OTHER ANIMAL
PLANKTON SHOWN HERE INCLUDE

TINY JELLYFISH AND CRAB LARVAE.
UNLIKE CRABS AND EELS,
COPEPODS DO NOT MATURE INTO
DIFFERENT FORMS, BUT REMAIN
PLANKTON ALL THEIR LIVES.

55

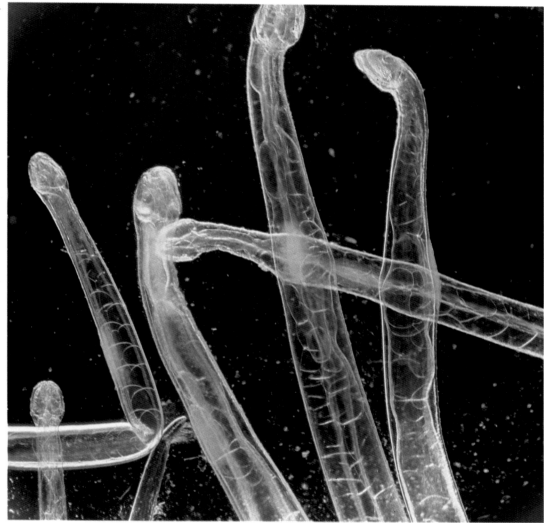

56

56 ARROW-WORMS

(Mike Laverack/Planet Earth)

SWARMING AMONGST PLANKTON, ARROW-WORMS ARE FEARSOME PREDATORS,
DEVOURING VAST QUANTITIES OF FISH EGGS – BUT THEY, IN TURN, ARE PREYED
UPON BY FISH. DIFFERENT SPECIES OF ARROW-WORMS ARE THE CLASSIC
'INDICATORS' FOR THE FISHERMEN OF SOUTHWEST ENGLAND: IN PAST DECADES
THE ABUNDANCE OF ONE SPECIES WAS LINKED TO THE PRESENCE OF HERRING,
BUT ANOTHER SPECIES WAS MOST ABUNDANT WHEN ANCHOVIES AND SARDINES
REPLACED THE HERRING.

57 A SEAL MOTHER AND HER PUP, SWIMMING

(Kim Westerskov)

IN MOST SEAL SPECIES THE FEMALES GIVE BIRTH A YEAR AFTER MATING, SO THAT THE YOUNG ARE BORN ON LAND, JUST BEFORE THE NEXT·BREEDING SEASON. THE PUPS ARE NURSED WHILE ON LAND, USUALLY FOR SEVERAL MONTHS. MOST SPECIES HAVE ACUTE HEARING, AND SOME MAKE USE OF SONAR FOR UNDERWATER NAVIGATION.

57

58

58 A CRAB-EATER SEAL, SWIMMING UNDER ICE

(Paul Drummond/B. & C. Alexander)

ALTHOUGH MOST SEALS ARE MAINLY FISH-EATERS, SOME, SUCH AS THE MISLEADINGLY NAMED CRAB-EATER SEAL OF THE ANTARCTIC, FEED ON KRILL AND OTHER ANIMAL PLANKTON.

59

59   A HUMPBACK WHALE FEEDING ON KRILL, ANTARCTICA
(Peter Scoones/Planet Earth)
DESPITE THEIR ENORMOUS SIZE, BALEEN WHALES SUCH AS THE HUMPBACK LIVE
ON ANIMAL PLANKTON, ESPECIALLY KRILL – SOMETIMES CONSUMING SEVERAL
TONNES A DAY. SWIMMING WITH THEIR MOUTHS OPEN, THEY FILTER THE KRILL
BY TAKING LARGE GULPS OF SEA-WATER, THEN EXPELLING IT THROUGH THE
FRINGES OF BALEEN (WHALEBONE) WHICH LINE THEIR MOUTHS. BEHIND THE
BALEEN 'STRAINER' VAST AMOUNTS OF KRILL ARE CAUGHT, WHICH THE WHALES
THEN SWALLOW.

**60 BLACK-BROWED ALBATROSSES
FEEDING IN THE SOUTH ATLANTIC**
(Peter J. Oxford/Planet Earth)
THE ALBATROSSES SEEN HERE ARE
SCAVENGING IN THE WAKE OF A
FISHING TRAWLER. THEY TOO
USUALLY EAT KRILL, WHICH
ABOUND IN THESE WATERS DURING
THE SUMMER. THE ABSENCE OF
VERTEBRATE PREDATORS, AND
THEIR ADAPTATION TO LIFE AT SEA,
FIT THESE BIRDS PERFECTLY FOR
POLAR REGIONS, WHERE THEY
ESTABLISH COLONIES ON REMOTE
SUB-ANTARCTIC ISLANDS.

61

**61 GREGARIOUS CHINSTRAP PENGUINS RALLYING ON AN ICEBERG, DECEPTION
ISLAND, ANTARCTICA**
(Ben Osborne)
LIKE THE BALEEN WHALES, ANTARCTIC PENGUINS FEED AT SEA ON KRILL. (WHEN
ON LAND THEY EAT NOTHING, SUBSISTING ON THE LAYER OF FAT UNDER THEIR
SKINS.) EVER SINCE WHALE NUMBERS BEGAN TO DECLINE SO DRAMATICALLY,
THERE HAS BEEN MORE AND MORE FOOD AVAILABLE FOR THESE BIRDS, AND
THEIR POPULATIONS HAVE INCREASED – A CLEAR DEMONSTRATION OF THE
INFLUENCE THAT ONE ORGANISM HAS ON ANOTHER IN THE FOOD WEB. ON LAND
PENGUINS WADDLE AWKWARDLY ON THEIR TWO LEGS, BUT ARE AGILE AND
GRACEFUL IN THE WATER.

69

68 CALIFORNIA SEA LIONS
(Richard Herrmann)
SEA LIONS ARE SUPERBLY ADAPTED
TO LIFE IN THE WATER, WITH THEIR
STRONG FLIPPERS AND SLEEK,
STREAMLINED BODIES WELL
COVERED BY A THICK LAYER OF
FAT, WHICH SERVES AS AN ENERGY
STORE AS WELL AS TO INSULATE.
SEA LIONS CAN DIVE RAPIDLY TO A
DEPTH OF UP TO 250 METRES (820
FT), AND MAY STAY SUBMERGED
FOR UP TO EIGHT MINUTES. THEY
INHABIT THE WATERS OF THE
SOUTHERN HEMISPHERE AND·THE
NORTH PACIFIC OCEAN.

70

**69 A SOUTHERN ELEPHANT SEAL,
ANTARCTICA**
(Gerry Ellis)
DURING THE NINETEENTH
CENTURY ELEPHANT SEALS WERE
HUNTED TO NEAR-EXTINCTION FOR
THEIR FUR, BUT THANKS TO
PROTECTIVE MEASURES THEIR
POPULATIONS ARE NOW RISING.

**70 A MOTHER HARP SEAL AND HER
PUP, GULF OF ST LAWRENCE**
(Heather Angel)
HARP SEALS DON'T EVEN VISIT
LAND TO BREED. FOR JUST TWO
WEEKS EARLY IN THE YEAR,
THOUSANDS OF FEMALES GATHER
ON THE 'WHELPING PATCHES' OF
THE ARCTIC ICE TO BEAR THEIR
YOUNG. THEN THE COLONY
MIGRATES TO WARMER WATERS,
WHERE THEY ALL DISPERSE UNTIL
THE NEXT BREEDING SEASON.

71

72

78

77 and 79 SALMON, CANADA (Gilbert
van Ryckevorsel/Planet Earth), **AND
LARVAE OF THE COMMON EEL**
(Heather Angel)
SOME FISH SPECIES MAKE
SPECTACULAR MIGRATIONS
BETWEEN FRESH WATER AND THE
SEA. SEA SALMON MAY TRAVEL 5,000
KM (OVER 3,000 MILES) TO THEIR
HOME STREAMS TO BREED; EELS
ARE SPAWNED IN THE SARGASSO
SEA BUT THEIR LARVAE MOVE WITH
OCEAN CURRENTS FOR THOUSANDS
OF KILOMETRES TO THE
FRESHWATER SHORES OF EUROPE
AND NORTH AMERICA. FIVE TO 15
YEARS LATER, THEY RETURN TO
THE SARGASSO TO BREED.

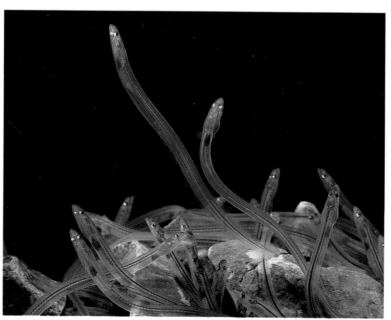

78 A GREEN TURTLE, BORNEO
(Linda Pitkin)
THE TURTLE LAYS ITS EGGS, AND
BURIES THEM, ON ANCESTRAL
HATCHING BEACHES ABOVE THE
HIGH-TIDE LINE. THE JUVENILES
HATCH ON SHORE, BUT
IMMEDIATELY HEAD FOR THE
OCEAN. LITTLE IS KNOWN ABOUT
WHERE THEY SPEND THEIR FIRST
FEW YEARS: IT'S ASSUMED THAT
THEY DRIFT WITH THE CURRENT,
FEEDING ON SMALL ANIMALS.
AFTER TWENTY OR THIRTY YEARS
THEY RETURN, BY REMARKABLE
FEATS OF NAVIGATION AND
MEMORY, TO BREED AT THE SITE
OF THEIR OWN HATCHING.

79

81

82

80, 81 and 82   ARCTIC TERNS (Norbert Rosing), **WHITE-TAILED TROPIC-BIRDS OF THE SEYCHELLES** (Mike Birkhead/OSF), **AND A SHEARWATER** (Kim Westerskov) ALL TERNS ARE SKILLED AND GRACEFUL FLIERS – SOME ARE ALSO CALLED 'SEA SWALLOWS'. THE ARCTIC TERN IS THE MOST REMARKABLE AVIAN VOYAGER OF ALL: IT FLIES POLE TO POLE TO CATCH BOTH POLAR SUMMERS. TROPIC-BIRDS ARE OCEAN TRAVELLERS SO SPECIALIZED THAT, THOUGH THEY ARE SUPERB SWIMMERS AND DIVERS, THEY CAN BARELY WALK, OR EVEN STAND, ON LAND. ALMOST ALWAYS IN THE WATER OR FLYING, SHEARWATERS GLIDE LOW ALONG WAVE TROUGHS IN SEARCH OF FISH. THEY COME TO LAND ONLY TO NEST AND RAISE THEIR CHICKS.

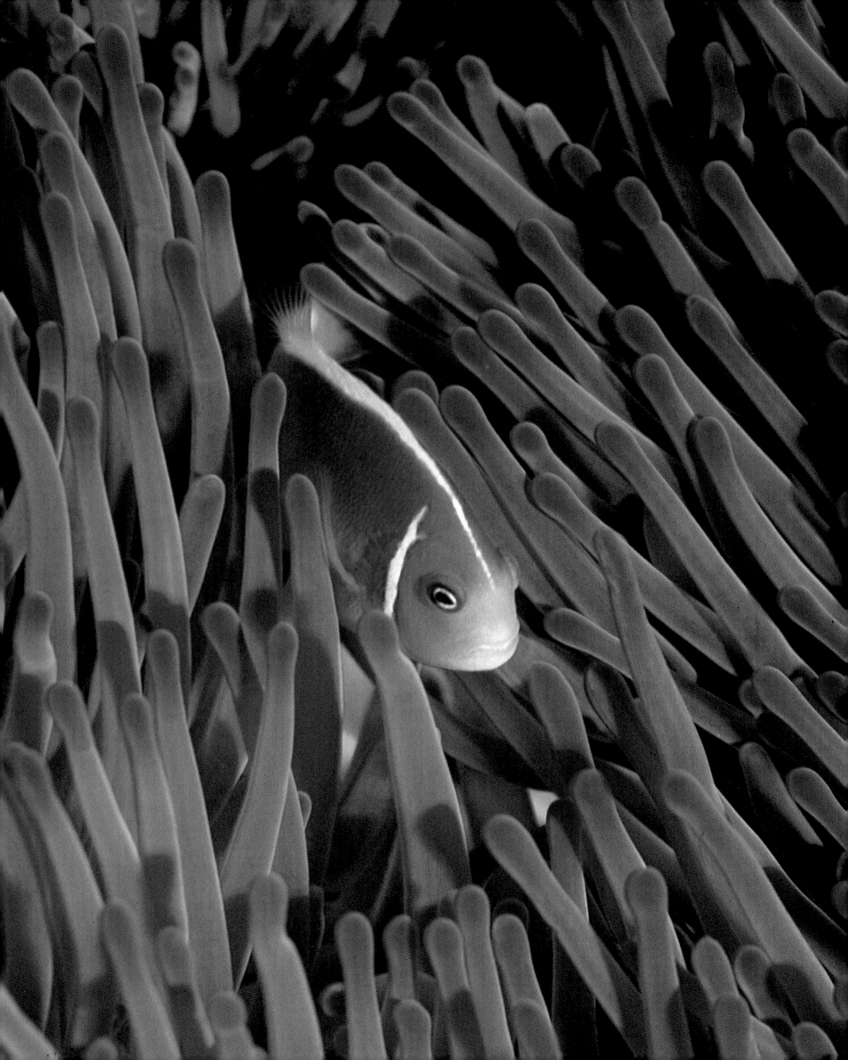

85

85   A HARLEQUIN TUSKFISH, BARRIER REEF, AUSTRALIA

(Norbert Wu)

THIS DAZZLING FISH IS COMMON ALL OVER THE REEF, EATING CRUSTACEANS
AND MOLLUSCS. IT IS A WRASSE, AND AS WITH ALL WRASSE – PARROTFISH,
GROUPERS, ANGELFISH AND OTHERS – SEX CHANGES OCCUR DURING THE LIFE
CYCLE OF SOME INDIVIDUALS: SOME FEMALES BECOME MALES. THESE
CHANGELING MALES ARE DOMINANT OVER OTHER MALES. WHILE THOSE BORN AS
MALES HAVE THE GAUDIEST COLOURING, 'CHANGED' FEMALES ARE SLIGHTLY
LESS ARRESTING, AND FEMALES AND JUVENILES ARE USUALLY DRAB.

86

**86 A QUEEN ANGELFISH,
CARIBBEAN**

(Norbert Wu)

A SINGLE MALE ANGELFISH
USUALLY LIVES WITH A HAREM OF
FEMALES. WHEN MATING, IT
NUZZLES THE FEMALE'S SIDE OR
BELLY FOR SEVERAL MINUTES
BEFORE THE PAIR SUDDENLY DASH
FOR THE SURFACE TO
SIMULTANEOUSLY RELEASE SPERM
AND THOUSANDS OF EGGS INTO
THE WATER.

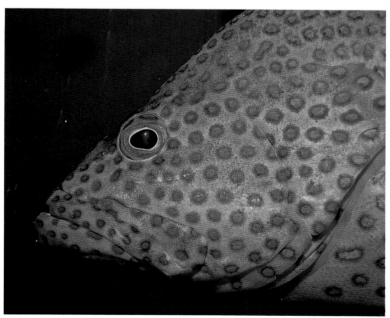

**87 A CORAL GROUPER, BARRIER
REEF, AUSTRALIA**

(Norbert Wu)

AS WITH ALL GROUPERS, SOME
FEMALES OF THIS SPECIES LATER
BECOME MALES; IN FACT, LARGER
AND OLDER CORAL GROUPERS ARE
PREDOMINANTLY MALES. SINCE
THE SPECIES IS FISHED FOR FOOD
AND BIGGER SPECIMENS ARE
PREFERRED, POPULATIONS MAY BE
LEFT WITHOUT ENOUGH MALES TO
SUCCESSFULLY REPRODUCE.

87

88

88   A SPOTTED CLEANER SHRIMP ON AN ANEMONE, GRAND CAYMAN
(J. Michael Kelly)
THIS SHRIMP, 1-2 CM (.4-1 IN) LONG, IS COMMON THROUGHOUT THE CARIBBEAN,
WHERE IT OFTEN LIVES WITHIN THE TENTACLES OF THE GIANT ANEMONE. IT
FEEDS BY SCOURING THE MOUTHS AND GILLS OF FISH FOR HARMFUL PARASITES.
THE ANEMONE AFFORDS IT PROTECTION FROM PREDATORS, WHILE THE SHRIMP
GAINS EXTRA NOURISHMENT BY FEEDING ON THE SCRAPS THAT THE ANEMONE
LEAVES. BEFORE THEY CAN INHABIT THE ANEMONE, SUCH SHRIMPS 'IMMUNIZE'
THEMSELVES BY PICKING AT THE TENTACLES FOR SEVERAL HOURS.

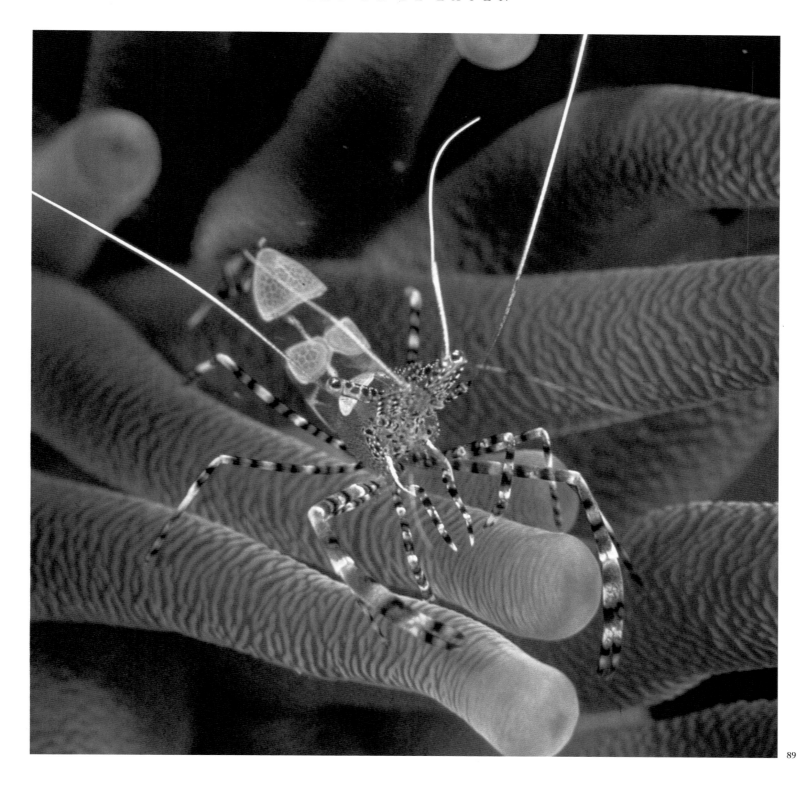

89

89 *PERICLIMENES YUCATANICUS* ON AN ANEMONE, CARIBBEAN

(B. Jones & M. Shimlock)

THIS CLEANER SHRIMP COHABITS WITH A VARIETY OF ANEMONES, WORKING
OVER THE TENTACLES AND BASE FOR DETRITUS. OCCASIONALLY IT CLEANS FISH
AS WELL, CONSUMING THE PARASITES IN THEIR GILLS AND MOUTHS. PERCHED
ON THE ANEMONE'S TENTACLES, IT WAVES ITS CLAWS IN ORDER TO ATTRACT THE
FISH TO THE 'CLEANING STATION'.

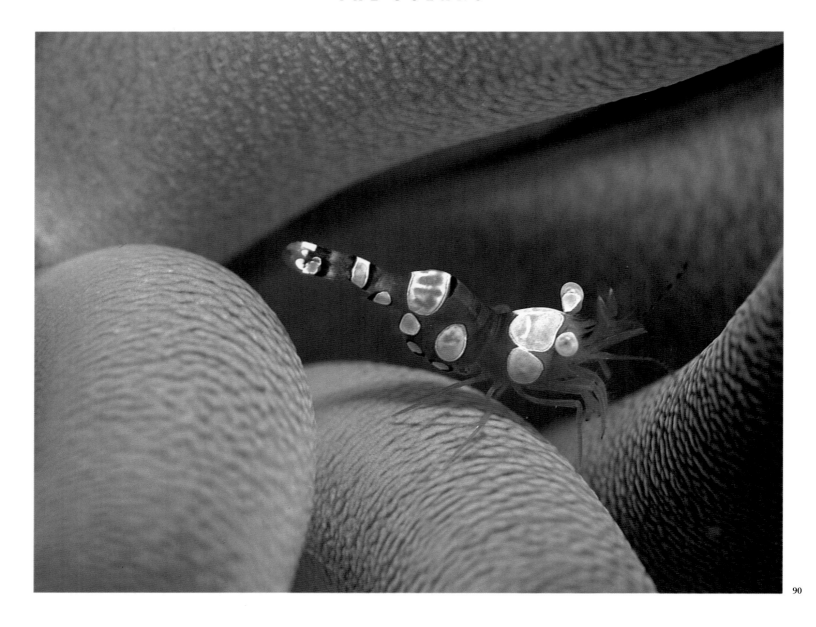

90

90   A SQUAT ANEMONE SHRIMP IN AN ANEMONE, LITTLE CAYMAN
(David Hall)
NOT ONE OF THE CLEANER SHRIMPS, THIS ONE GROWS TO A MAXIMUM 1 CM (.4
IN). IT IS SHY, AND WILL RETREAT INTO THE TENTACLES WHEN APPROACHED.
SOME SHRIMP SPECIES ARE NEVER FOUND SEPARATE FROM ANEMONES – THEIR
RELATIONSHIP WITH THEIR HOST IS OBLIGATE.

91   ANOTHER *PERICLIMENES* ON AN ANEMONE, SIPADAN, MALAYSIA
(B. Jones & M. Shimlock)
THIS TINY SHRIMP, ALSO RATHER SELF-EFFACING, HELPS NOT FISH, BUT ITS
ANEMONE HOST, TO STAY CLEAN. RATHER THAN RESTING ON THE TENTACLES, IT
ENTERS THE ACTUAL MOUTH OF THE ANEMONE TO REACH ITS INNER PARTS.

92

92 A HERMIT CRAB ON FIRE
CORAL, IN THE RED SEA AT NIGHT
(Jeffrey L. Rotman)
HERMIT CRABS ARE FOUND IN
SHALLOW COASTAL WATERS
THROUGHOUT THE WORLD, BUT
ESPECIALLY AMONG CORAL REEFS.
RATHER THAN MANUFACTURING
ITS OWN SHELL, THE SOFT-BODIED
HERMIT FINDS AND WEARS ONE
THAT ANOTHER CREATURE HAS
DISCARDED; WHEN IT HAS
OUTGROWN IT, THE HERMIT
EXCHANGES IT FOR ANOTHER.
HERMITS OFTEN SHARE THEIR
SHELLS WITH OPOSSUM SHRIMPS
AND THEIR YOUNG – THE GUESTS
MAY HELP TO KEEP THE SHELL
CLEAN.

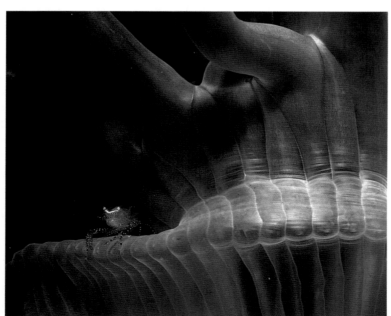

93

93 A CLEANER SHRIMP ON THE
BASAL DISC OF AN ANEMONE, RED
SEA
(Jeffrey L. Rotman)
A SHRIMP'S EXOSKELETON DOES
NOT PROVIDE PROTECTION
AGAINST THE ANEMONE'S STING.
LIKE CLOWN-FISH, WHICH ALSO
LIVE AMONGST ANEMONES, THE
SHRIMP APPEARS TO ACCLIMATIZE
ITSELF TO THE STING, AND LIVES
UNHARMED WITHIN ITS HOST.

94

94   A CHAMBERED NAUTILUS, VANUATU, SOUTH PACIFIC OCEAN
(David Hall)
THE NAUTILUS IS ONE OF THE MOST PRIMITIVE CREATURES IN THE SEAS TODAY,
A SURVIVOR OF SOME 500 MILLION YEARS, AND FOUND THROUGHOUT THE INDO-
PACIFIC OCEANS. IT INHABITS DEEP WATERS (UP TO 700 METRES, 2,300 FT) DURING
THE DAY, BUT MIGRATES TO FEED IN SHALLOWER WATERS (30-60 METRES, 100-200
FT) BY NIGHT. IT CONTROLS ITS BUOYANCY – ITS ASCENT AND DESCENT – BY
REGULATING THE PROPORTIONS OF GAS AND WATER IN THE CHAMBERS OF ITS
SPECIALIZED SHELL.

95

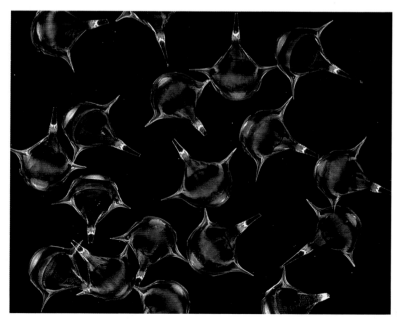

96

95   OSTRACODS (*VARGULA CYPRIDINA*)

(P.J. Herring/IOS)

THESE 2-2.5 MM (ABOUT 0.1 IN) LONG, DETRITUS-CONSUMING CREATURES INHABIT CORAL REEFS IN THE INDO-PACIFIC AREA. DURING THE DAY THEY HIDE AWAY AMONGST THE CORAL AND IN THE SEDIMENT. THEN AT NIGHT THEY SWIM TO THE SURFACE, SETTING THE OCEAN ALIGHT WITH THEIR EERIE BLUE LUMINESCENCE, WHICH THEY RELEASE INTO THE WATER FROM GLANDS ON THEIR UPPER LIPS.

96   PTEROPODS, *DIACRIA MAJOR*, NORTH EAST ATLANTIC

(Heather Angel)

THESE TINY 'WINGED' MOLLUSCS GENERALLY FUNCTION FIRST AS MALES AND THEN AS FEMALES, LAYING GELATINOUS MASSES OF STICKY EGGS. BUT WHEN FOOD IS SCARCE AND ENERGY CANNOT BE EXPENDED ON SEXUAL REPRODUCTION, THEY BECOME HERMAPHRODITES, SHEDDING THEIR SHELLS, SHRINKING IN SIZE AND SPLITTING INTO SEVERAL ANIMALS.

97

97 A SQUID, *LOLIGO OPALESCENS*, AND ITS EGGS, CALIFORNIA
(Richard Herrmann)
NAMED *OPALESCENS* FOR ITS IRIDESCENT EYES, THIS SQUID SPAWNS IN VAST NUMBERS IN MONTEREY BAY, SOUTH OF SAN FRANCISCO. IT SPAWNS JUST ONCE IN ITS LIFETIME, AND THEN DIES. INVESTING HARD-WON ENERGY IN A SINGLE BURST OF REPRODUCTION IS A COMMON STRATEGY AMONG MARINE ANIMALS.

98 OCTOPUS EGGS HATCHING
(Norbert Wu)
LIKE SQUID (97), OCTOPUSES SPAWN JUST ONCE BEFORE DYING. THE YOUNG LOOK JUST LIKE ADULTS, BUT MEASURE A MERE 3 CM (1 IN APPROX.) INCLUDING THEIR TENTACLES. OCTOPUSES SPAWN *EN MASSE*, BUT DIVIDE THE AVAILABLE SEA-FLOOR SPACE INTO TERRITORIES – CLUSTERS OF EGGS ARE SEEN AT REGULAR INTERVALS. TERRITORY IS ALL-IMPORTANT FOR THE HATCHING YOUNG, WHICH GROW RAPIDLY. THE BEST SPOTS, PROVIDING PLENTY OF FOOD, ARE AT THE CENTRE OF THE MASS; AT THE OUTSKIRTS, THE OFFSPRING ARE VULNERABLE TO PREDATORS AND MAY FIND FOOD HARD TO COME BY.

98

99

99   A BLACK SWALLOWER, WITH PREY

(Norbert Wu)

IN THE DEEP SEA WHERE THIS FISH LIVES, FOOD IS SCARCE AND ANY
OPPORTUNITY MUST BE SEIZED. MANY ANIMALS ARE CAPABLE OF EATING PREY AS
LARGE AS THEMSELVES – A CASE OF 'EAT, OR BE EATEN'. SUCH CREATURES MAY
FEED ONLY ONCE EVERY FEW MONTHS; THEIR STOMACHS TAKE TIME TO DIGEST
THE FOOD, WHICH PROVIDES A SLOW-RELEASE ENERGY STORE.

100   DEEP-SEA ANGLERFISH, *LINOPHRYNE INDICA*: A FEMALE AND A DWARF MALE

(Norbert Wu)

MANY TIMES BIGGER THAN THE MALE ANGLERFISH, BUT SLUGGISH AND POORLY
SIGHTED, THE FEMALE ATTEMPTS TO DEVOUR HIM WHEN HE APPROACHES HER.
BUT, WITH HIS AGILITY AND SUPERIOR VISION, HE USUALLY MANAGES TO FASTEN
HIMSELF TO HER SIDE WITH HIS LITTLE JAWS BEFORE SHE HAS A CHANCE TO
GOBBLE HIM UP. HIS MOUTH SOON FUSES WITH HER SKIN AND EVENTUALLY
THEIR CIRCULATORY SYSTEMS MERGE. NOW ESSENTIALLY A SACK OF SPERM, THE
MALE RECEIVES ALL HIS NUTRIENTS VIA HIS HOSTESS. IN THE EMPTY DEPTHS OF
THE OCEAN, THIS STRATEGY ENSURES THAT THEY WILL BE TOGETHER WHEN THE
FEMALE IS READY TO BREED.

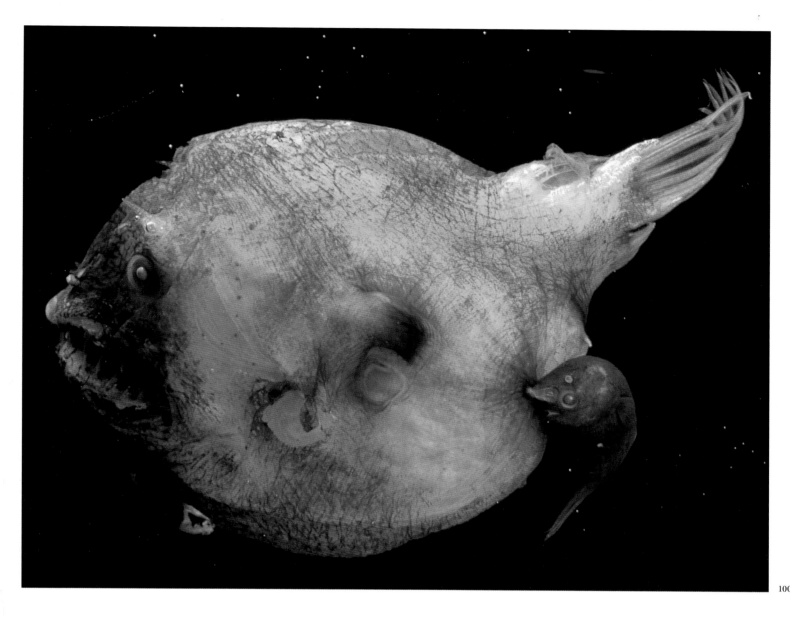

100

**101   A DEEP-SEA ANGLERFISH
LARVA, CELEBES SEA, INDONESIA**
(Norbert Wu)
ANGLERFISH BEGIN THEIR LIVES AS
LARVAE DWELLING CLOSE TO THE
SEA'S SURFACE, WHERE FOOD IS
PLENTIFUL. THE BUBBLE-LIKE
STRUCTURE AROUND THE LARVA
(SHOWN HERE) IS A BUOYANCY
DEVICE. AS IT BEGINS TO
METAMORPHOSE INTO THE ADULT
FORM, IT WILL MIGRATE TO THE
DEPTHS, WHERE IT WILL SPEND
THE REST OF ITS LIFE.

101

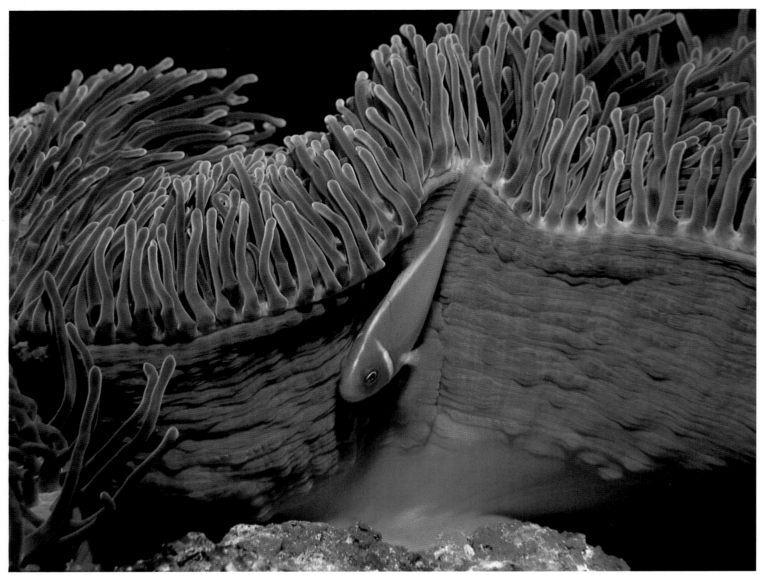

104

105

106

104   A CLOWN-FISH ON AN ANEMONE, SOLOMON ISLANDS

(David Hall)

THERE ARE 26 SPECIES OF CLOWN-FISH, INHABITING 10 SPECIES OF ANEMONE.
THESE VERY COLOURFUL FISH, WHICH LIVE ON CORAL REEFS, ARE
HERMAPHRODITIC – ALL ARE BORN AS MALES, BUT SOME LATER CHANGE INTO
FEMALES. THE FEMALES, WHICH ARE LARGER, ARE THE BOSSES.

105   A BALLED ANEMONE, SOLOMON ISLANDS

(B. Jones & M. Shimlock)

WHY ANEMONES 'BALL UP', OR RETRACT, IS NOT CERTAIN. USUALLY IF ONE IS IN
THAT STATE, SO ARE ITS NEAR NEIGHBOURS. BALLING UP MAY BE A REACTION TO
LOW TIDES OR LOW LIGHT, OR A WAY OF PROTECTING THE MOUTH DISC;
ALTERNATIVELY, THE ANEMONE MAY RETRACT IN ORDER TO UNCOVER THE
CORAL AROUND THE BASE WHEN ITS SYMBIOTIC FISH BEGIN TO SPAWN AND LAY
THEIR EGGS THERE.

106   A CLOWN-FISH, *AMPHIPRION FRENATUS*, IN AN ANEMONE, PHILIPPINES

(David Hall)

CLOWN-FISH APPEAR GRADUALLY TO BUILD UP AN IMMUNITY TO THE ANEMONES'
STING, BY MAKING REPEATED SHORT CONTACT, USUALLY STARTING WITH THE
TAIL. ALSO, THEIR COATING OF SLIME MAY PROTECT THEM.

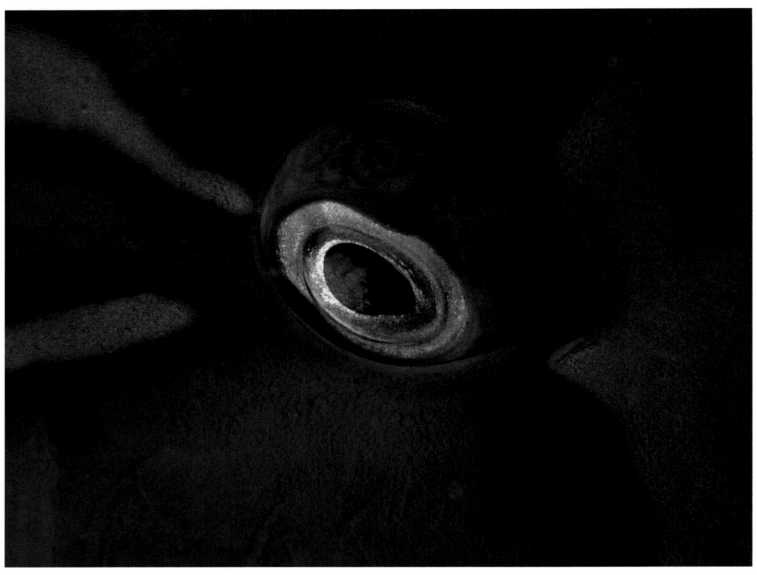

107

107, 108 and 109   **PARROTFISH EYES** (B. Jones & M. Shimlock)
AND A PUFFERFISH EYE (B. Jones & M. Shimlock)
THE EYES OF MANY CORAL REEF FISH LIKE THESE ARE EXTREMELY SENSITIVE TO
COLOUR, WHICH MAY BE USED TO ATTRACT, WARN OR ADVERTISE. THIS IS IN
MARKED CONTRAST TO THE EYES OF FISH LIVING DEEPER DOWN IN THE OCEAN,
WHERE LIGHT IS LOW: THERE, MOST FISH HAVE NO COLOUR VISION, AND THEIR
EYES ARE TUNED TO BLUE ONLY.

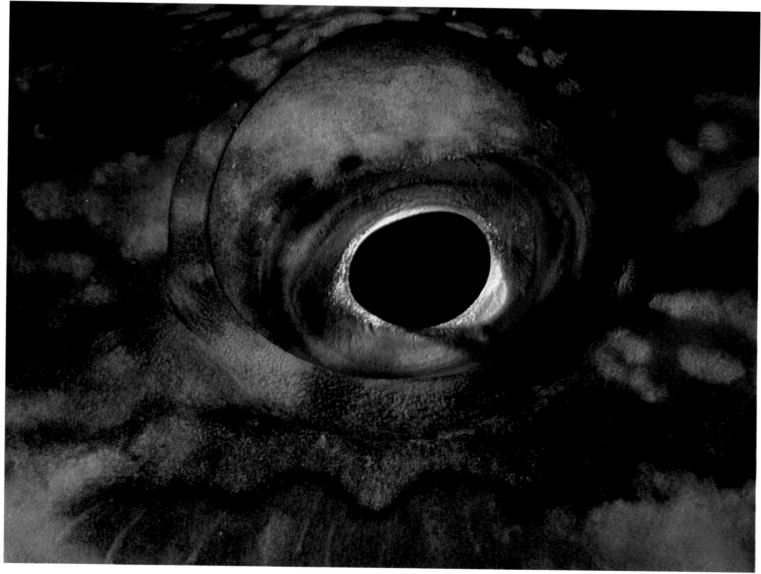

108

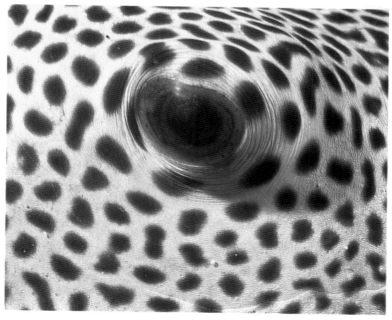

109

110

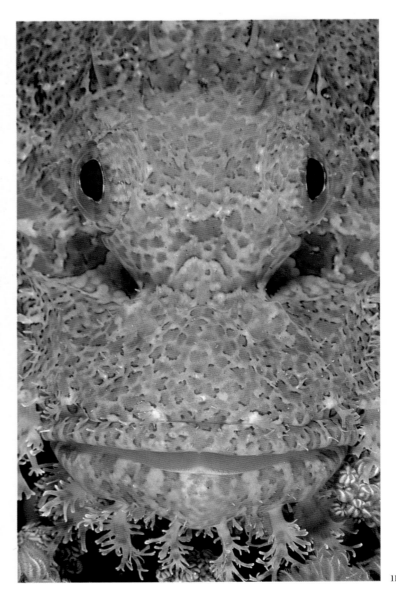

111

112

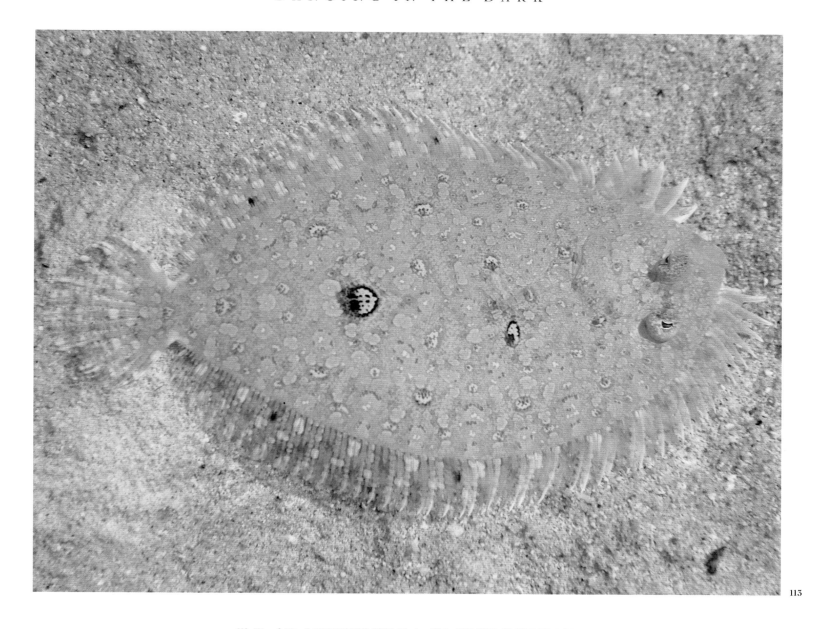

113

110, 111 and 112   A CROCODILE-FISH (Norbert Wu), **AND TWO SCORPION-FISH**

(B. Jones & M. Shimlock)

THE 'HAIRY' GROWTHS AND MOTTLED COLOURING OF THESE REEF INHABITANTS
BLEND ALMOST PERFECTLY WITH THEIR CORAL BACKGROUND. SCORPION-FISH,
UNLIKE CROCODILE-FISH **(110)**, ARE HIGHLY POISONOUS AND CAN GIVE A PAINFUL,
EVEN FATAL, STING IF INADVERTENTLY TRODDEN ON. THEY ARE MAINLY
NOCTURNAL. BY DAY THEIR SUPERB CAMOUFLAGE CONCEALS THEM FROM
PREDATORS AND FROM PREY; BY NIGHT THEY WAIT TO POUNCE ON INCAUTIOUS
VICTIMS.

113   A PEACOCK FLOUNDER, GRAND CAYMAN

(J. Michael Kelly)

MOST FLATFISH LIKE THIS FLOUNDER CAN MERGE INDISTINGUISHABLY WITH THE
SAND OR MUD OF THE SEABED WHERE MOST OF THEM LIVE. MANY ADULTS
ADAPT THE COLOUR OF THEIR PIGMENTED UPPER SIDE TO MATCH THAT OF THE
SEA FLOOR. IDEALLY HIDDEN IN THIS WAY, THESE CARNIVORES LIE IN WAIT FOR
SMALL CRUSTACEANS AND OTHER PREY, WHICH THEY LOCATE WITH THEIR KEEN
SENSE OF SMELL.

114

114   AN ATLANTIC COMB-JELLY AND A JELLYFISH
(Peter Parks/Norbert Wu Photography)

COMB-JELLIES ARE GELATINOUS PLANKTONIC ORGANISMS, NUMBERING ABOUT 90 SPECIES WIDELY DISTRIBUTED IN THE WORLD'S OCEANS. THEY FEED ON SMALLER PLANKTON AND ARE THEMSELVES PREYED ON BY FISH. THEIR BODIES ARE LITTLE MORE THAN A THIN CASE AROUND A CAVITY. BUT THE CAVITY IS IN FACT A HUGE PLANKTON TRAP: ON ENCOUNTERING THEIR PREY, THEY 'VACUUM' IT UP. ONE SPECIES, FOUND IN THE WEST ATLANTIC, IS THOUGHT TO SWALLOW NEARLY 500 COPEPODS EVERY HOUR. COMB-JELLIES HAVE NO TENTACLES, AND SWIM MOUTH FIRST. TWO ROWS OF HAIR-LIKE CILIA BEAT SYNCHRONOUSLY TO PROPEL THEM ALONG. MANY COMB-JELLIES AND JELLYFISH, LIKE THOSE SHOWN HERE, ARE LUMINESCENT. THE JELLYFISH IS ABOUT THE SIZE OF A FIST AND IS OF AN EXCEPTIONALLY BRIGHT-SHINING KIND. JELLYFISH RANGE FROM THE OCEAN SURFACE TO ALMOST ANY DEPTH, AND FROM TROPICAL WATERS TO SUBPOLAR.

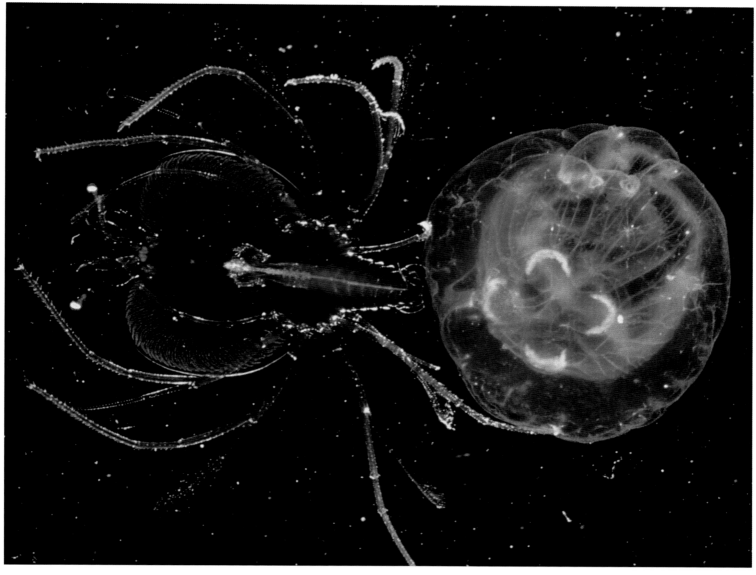

115

115   A LOBSTER LARVA HITCHING A LIFT WITH A MOON JELLY
(Peter Parks/Norbert Wu Photography)
AT LARVAL STAGE, THE WEAK-SWIMMING, TRANSPARENT LOBSTER BEARS LITTLE
RELATION TO ITS ADULT FORM. BEFORE THEY SETTLE ON THE SEABED AND
BEGIN TO LOOK LIKE LOBSTERS AS WE KNOW THEM, THE LARVAE SWIM ABOUT IN
THE PLANKTON FOR A YEAR OR MORE, MOULTING BETWEEN 14 AND 17 TIMES. BUT
BEFORE THEY ARE READY TO SEARCH FOR A SUITABLE PLACE ON THE SEA FLOOR
TO METAMORPHOSE, A HUGE NUMBER OF LARVAE ARE LOST. FOR, APART FROM
THEIR TRANSPARENCY, THEY ARE COMPLETELY UNPROTECTED AGAINST A WIDE
VARIETY OF ENEMIES, FROM WHICH THEY HAVE LITTLE CHANCE OF ESCAPE.
ABOUT 10 PER CENT OF A LARVAL OYSTER SWARM, FOR INSTANCE, IS EATEN EACH
DAY. IN ADDITION, THE LARVAE PREY ON EACH OTHER. CRAB LARVAE FEED ON
LARVAL MOLLUSCS, AND ARE THEMSELVES DEVOURED BY LOBSTER LARVAE.
SOMETIMES LARVAE HITCH A LIFT WITH OTHER ORGANISMS, GAINING EFFORT-
FREE TRANSPORT THROUGH THE SEAS.

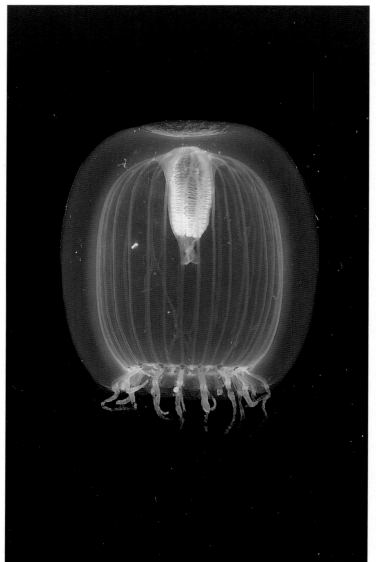

116

117

118

119

116, 117 and 118   LUMINOUS JELLYFISH

(IOS; Norbert Wu; Jeffrey L. Rotman)

MANY JELLYFISH HAVE COLOURED INTERNAL STRUCTURES VISIBLE THROUGH A
TRANSPARENT OR DELICATELY TINTED BELL. SOME PRODUCE GLOWS OR FLASHES
WHEN THEY ARE TOUCHED BY ANOTHER ANIMAL – PROBABLY AS A DEFENCE
MECHANISM INTENDED TO ALARM OR WARN PREDATORS. INTERESTINGLY,
JELLYFISH CANNOT SEE THEIR OWN DISPLAYS, SO THESE REACTIONS HAVE
EVOLVED IN RESPONSE TO OTHERS' EYES.

119   AN ANGLERFISH

(IOS)

THE *MELANOCETUS* ANGLERFISH IS A DEEP-LIVING SPECIES THAT HAS EVOLVED A
SPECIALLY MODIFIED DORSAL FIN – A 'FISHING ROD', WITH ITS LUMINOUS LIGHT
ORGAN AT THE END, ACTING AS 'BAIT'; IN THIS WAY, IT 'CATCHES' SMALL FISH,
SQUID AND CRUSTACEANS. ONCE THE FEROCIOUS TEETH HAVE CLAMPED DOWN
ON THEIR VICTIMS, ONLY THE TINIEST STAND A CHANCE OF SLIPPING BACK INTO
THE WATER.

120

120   A DEEP-SEA HATCHET-FISH
(Norbert Wu/OSF)

121   A DEEP-LIVING DECAPOD: *EPHYRINA FIGUERIAE*
(Heather Angel)
THIS CREATURE LIVES AT A DEPTH OF ABOUT 1,000 METRES (3,300 FT). BELOW
ABOUT 600 METRES (1,970 FT), MOST ORGANISMS ARE EITHER RED OR BLACK. SINCE
RED IS INVISIBLE AT THESE DEPTHS, IT SERVES AS A CAMOUFLAGE. THE RED
COLOUR RESULTS FROM ACCUMULATED CAROTENOID PIGMENTS, ORIGINALLY
DERIVED FROM PLANT PLANKTON. MOST DEEP-SEA DECAPODS, INCLUDING THIS
SPECIES, EMIT DISGUISING CLOUDS OF LUMINESCENT FLUID WHEN A PREDATOR
DISTURBS THEM.

122   A FLASHLIGHT FISH, INDIAN OCEAN
(Norbert Wu)
THIS DEEP-SEA FISH HAS A LARGE 'HEADLIGHT' BENEATH ITS EYE. THE LIGHT
SOURCE IS NOT ELECTRICAL, BUT DERIVES FROM LUMINESCENT BACTERIA
INHABITING THE LIGHT ORGAN, WHICH THE FISH USES FOR THE PURPOSE OF
ILLUMINATING PREY.

121

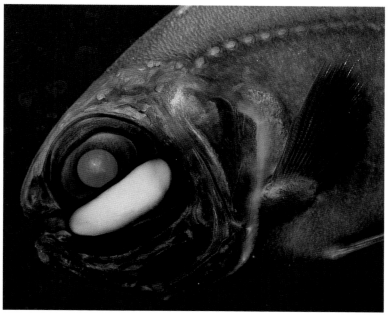

122

125

126

127

125, 126 and 127   WAVES
(Tony Stone Worldwide; Paul Berger/Tony Stone Worldwide; Warren Bolster/Tony Stone Worldwide)
CARBON DIOXIDE IN THE ATMOSPHERE DISSOLVES IN THE SEA'S CONSTANTLY
CHURNING SURFACE, TO BE TAKEN UP BY PLANT PLANKTON AND USED IN
PHOTOSYNTHESIS. DEAD PLANKTON SINK DOWN DEEP INTO THE OCEAN AS
SMALL CLUMPS. SOME ANIMAL PLANKTON ARE MIGRATING GRAZERS, THAT RISE
AT NIGHT TO FEED, THEN BY DAY DESCEND, AND RELEASE THE CARBON DIOXIDE.
THUS THE SEAS ACT AS A CARBON DIOXIDE SINK, AND ARE CONTINUALLY
DRAWING ATMOSPHERIC CARBON DIOXIDE INTO THEIR WATERS. CONSEQUENTLY,
THE AMOUNT OF THIS GAS IN THE SEAS GREATLY EXCEEDS THE AMOUNT IN THE
ATMOSPHERE. WITHOUT THIS EFFECT, ATMOSPHERIC CONCENTRATIONS WOULD
BE FAR HIGHER, AND GLOBAL TEMPERATURES WOULD SOAR.

128

128, 129 and 130   ICEBERGS, ANTARCTICA
(Ben Osborne)
WHEN A GLACIER BRINGS ICE TO THE SEA, LARGE BLOCKS BREAK OFF INTO THE
WATER, FORMING ICEBERGS. THIS PROCESS IS CALLED 'CALVING'. ONLY ABOUT
ONE NINTH OF AN ICEBERG'S TOTAL MASS PROJECTS ABOVE THE WATER. JUST AS
A RIVER CARRIES ITS HEAVIEST LOAD IN THE SPRING, SO DOES A GLACIER. THE
ICEBERG 'SEASON' OCCURS IN APRIL IN THE NORTHERN HEMISPHERE AND IN
OCTOBER IN THE SOUTHERN. BY STUDYING THE GRAVEL AND ROCKS THAT HAVE
GRADUALLY FALLEN TO THE SEABED AS ICEBERGS MELT, SCIENTISTS HAVE BEEN
ABLE TO DISCOVER THE FULL EXTENT OF ICEBERGS DURING GLACIATIONS.
GREENLAND IS THE SOURCE OF MOST OF THE ICEBERGS IN THE NORTH ATLANTIC.
THE LAST ICE AGE STARTED ABOUT 85,000 YEARS AGO AND PEAKED SOME 18,000
YEARS AGO. IT WAS THE LATEST IN A SERIES OF GLACIATIONS THAT STARTED
ABOUT ONE AND A HALF MILLION YEARS AGO. CHANGES IN THE SUN'S OUTPUT,
'GREENHOUSE' GASES, OCEANIC CIRCULATION – EVEN DUSTCLOUDS FROM
MASSIVE VOLCANIC ERUPTIONS – HAVE BEEN VARIOUSLY IMPLICATED AS CAUSES.
THE BURNING OF FOSSIL FUELS BY HUMANS MAY HAVE BROUGHT THIS CYCLE TO
AN END. WE CANNOT YET KNOW WHAT THE CONSEQUENCES WILL BE.

129

130

131

132

133

131, 132 and 133 SANDFLAT SEDIMENT (Laurie Campbell), **ACORN BARNACLES**
(Laurie Campbell), **AND URCHIN SKELETONS** (B. Jones & M. Shimlock)
SEA SHELLS ARE FORMED MAINLY OF CALCIUM CARBONATE, A MINERAL PRESENT
IN SEA-WATER, THOUGH THE SHELLS OF SOME MICROSCOPIC PLANT PLANKTON
ARE ALSO MANUFACTURED FROM SILICA. WHEN SHALLOW-WATER ANIMALS DIE,
THEIR HARD CASES ARE POUNDED INTO SEDIMENT BY THE WAVES. SIMILARLY, IN
DEEP WATER, THE SKELETONS OF MICROSCOPIC PLANT AND ANIMAL PLANKTON
ACCUMULATE INTO SEDIMENT. GRADUALLY, THEY ARE COVERED OVER BY FRESH
SEDIMENT; AFTER MILLIONS OF YEARS' COMPRESSION AND DRYING THEY WILL
FORM NEW ROCK.

134 KELP ON ROCKS AT LOW TIDE
(Kim Westerskov)
A LARGE PROPORTION OF THE
VITAL MINERALS FOUND IN SEA-
WATER ARE DERIVED FROM LAND,
ERODED FROM ROCKS BY THE
CEASELESS PASSAGE OF RIVERS
FLOWING INTO THE SEA.

141

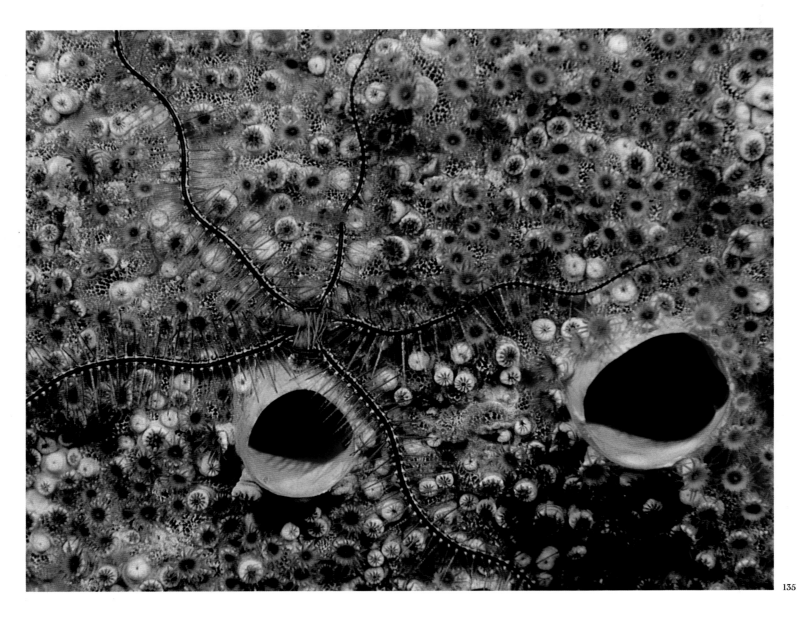

135

135 and 136 ENCRUSTING SPONGES
(J. Michael Kelly; Linda Pitkin)
SPONGES FILTER-FEED ON THE
RAIN OF SEDIMENT FROM DEAD
PLANTS AND ANIMALS LIVING AT
THE OCEAN SURFACE. THESE
PRIMITIVE ANIMALS COME IN MANY
FORMS, BUT OFTEN ENCRUST SOLID
MASSES SUCH AS REEFS AND
ROCKS.

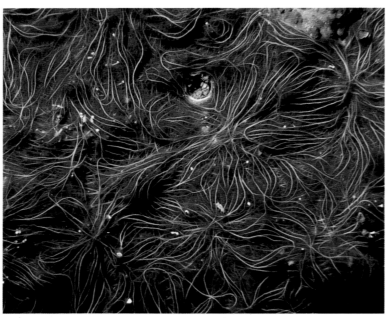

136

**137 AN AZURE VASE SPONGE,
LITTLE CAYMAN**
(David Hall)
SPONGES ARE ESSENTIALLY SIMPLE
AGGREGATIONS OF CELLS
ENCLOSING A SYSTEM OF CANALS
THROUGH WHICH WATER IS
PUMPED, BRINGING FOOD AND
OXYGEN AND REMOVING WASTE.
THEIR SHAPE IS LARGELY
GOVERNED BY THE WATER
CURRENTS WHERE THEY GROW.
WHERE WATER IS LIABLE TO MOVE
WITH FORCE, A ROUNDED CLUMP
OFFERS LESS RESISTANCE, BUT IN
TRANQUIL WATERS SHAPES MAY BE
MORE DELICATE.

139

138   A JORDAN'S PRAWN, CALIFORNIA

(Richard Herrmann)

PRAWNS OF THE *PANDALUS* SPECIES ARE BOTTOM-LIVING OMNIVORES, AND
MOVE IN LARGE SWARMS. THEY ARE MOST OFTEN FOUND ON ORGANIC-RICH
SEDIMENTS, FORAGING FOR CARRION AND PLANT DEBRIS.

139   A SPONGE CRAB, INDONESIA

(Linda Pitkin)

MOST CRABS ARE CARNIVORES AND DETRITUS-FEEDERS, SIFTING THROUGH
THE ORGANIC DEBRIS OF THE OCEAN FLOOR OR COASTLINE. SPONGE CRABS
ARE HOST TO SPONGES WHICH GROW ON THEIR SHELLS. IN THIS SYMBIOTIC
RELATIONSHIP THE CRAB ACQUIRES NOT ONLY CAMOUFLAGE BUT
PROTECTION TOO, SINCE MANY OF THE SPONGES ARE DISTASTEFUL OR
TOXIC. THE SPONGE, IN EXCHANGE, GAINS MOBILITY AND, BECAUSE CRABS
ARE MESSY EATERS, IT ALSO GETS A SHARE OF THE FOOD THE CRUSTACEAN
SCATTERS.

140

141

140 GOOSE BARNACLES

(IOS)

THESE SMALL CRUSTACEANS DRIFT ALONG WITH THE CURRENT, ATTACHED TO
FLOATING OBJECTS. SOME SPECIES OF GOOSE BARNACLE ATTACH THEMSELVES
TO SHIPS, AND OTHERS TO WHALES. THE LARVAE FASTEN THEMSELVES ON WITH
AN ADHESIVE SECRETED BY A 'CEMENT GLAND', AND WITHIN JUST TEN DAYS
THEY HAVE MATURED. WITH THEIR FROND-LIKE TENTACLES, THEY CATCH
WHATEVER COMES THEIR WAY, SCAVENGING PLANT AND ANIMAL FRAGMENTS
FROM THE WATER.

141 FAN-WORMS, CARIBBEAN

(Norbert Wu)

FAN-WORMS LIVE IN COLONIES ATTACHED TO ROCKS AND CORAL. THEIR BODIES
END IN A CROWN OF FAN-LIKE FRONDS, WHICH FILTER FINE PARTICLES
INCLUDING PLANKTON FROM THE WATER BUT ALSO SERVE AS THE ANIMALS'
GILLS. THE CROWNS RAPIDLY CONTRACT IF TOUCHED.

142

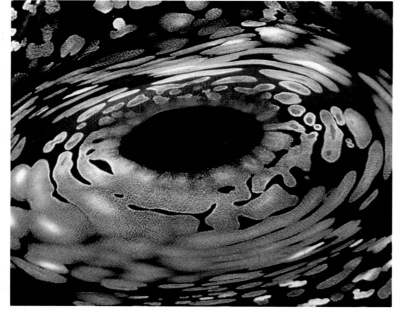

143

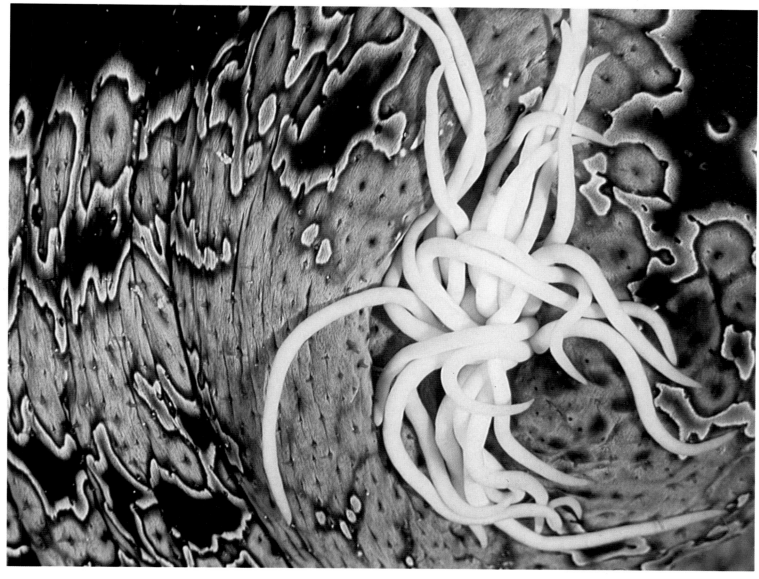

144

142 and 143   THE GIANT CLAM: DETAIL OF A MANTLE (David Hall),
AND A SYPHON (David Hall)

FORMERLY WIDESPREAD IN TROPICAL WATERS, GIANT CLAMS ARE NOW
THREATENED BY HUMANS HUNTING THEM FOR THEIR FLESH AND THEIR SHELLS.
THEY GROW UP TO A METRE (3 FT) IN DIAMETER. CLAMS FEED BY EXTRACTING
ORGANIC PARTICLES FROM THE WATER THAT THEY SIPHON THROUGH THEIR
MOUTHPARTS. PHOTOSYNTHESIZING ALGAE LIVE IN THEIR MANTLES, AND
PROVIDE THEM WITH ADDITIONAL ENERGY.

144   A SEA CUCUMBER EVISCERATING, FIJI
· (B. Jones & M. Shimlock)

SEA CUCUMBERS ARE A LARGE GROUP OF SOFT, SAUSAGE-SHAPED ANIMALS THAT
FEED ON DEBRIS AMONG THE MUD OR SAND OF THE SEA FLOOR, WHERE MOST
SPECIES LIVE. WHEN ATTACKED, THEY SOMETIMES EVISCERATE, OR THROW OUT
THEIR INTERNAL ORGANS, WHICH ARE STICKY, AND DISTASTEFUL TO THE
PREDATOR. THE ORGANS REGENERATE.

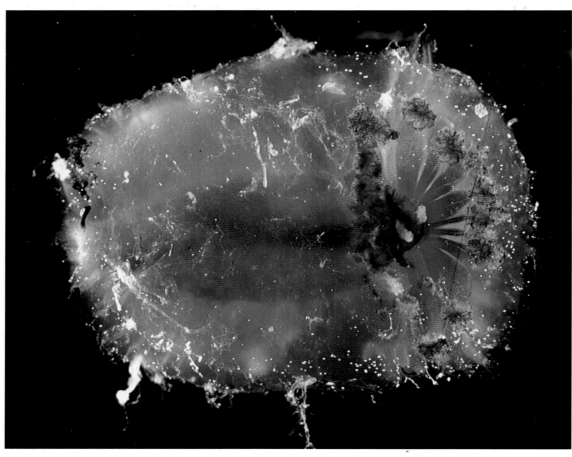

145

146

145 and 146   A LUMINOUS SEA
CUCUMBER (IOS), AND A FEMALE
OSTRACOD, WITH EGGS (IOS)
BOTH OF THESE DEEP-SEA
CREATURES LIVE OFF THE DEBRIS
LEFT BEHIND AFTER MORE
SHALLOW-WATER ANIMALS HAVE
FINISHED SCAVENGING. THOUGH IT
IS SOMETIMES FOUND CLOSER TO
THE SURFACE, THIS SEA CUCUMBER
IS AT HOME AT DEPTHS OF 5,000
METRES (OVER 3 MILES). THE
SYMBIOTIC BACTERIA THAT
INHABIT ITS TENTACLES MAY HELP
IT TO DIGEST FOOD. THE
OSTRACOD, A SMALL CRUSTACEAN,
LIVES AT DEPTHS OF 3,000 METRES
(ALMOST 2 MILES) AND MORE. THE
PINK BALLS VISIBLE HERE ARE ITS
EGGS.

147   THE DEEP-SEA CRUSTACEAN,
EURYTHENES GRYLLUS
(IOS)
THE 'BLUEBOTTLE' OF THE OCEANS:
IT AVIDLY DEVOURS CORPSES AND
OTHER DEBRIS THAT SINK TO THE
SEA FLOOR WHERE IT LIVES.

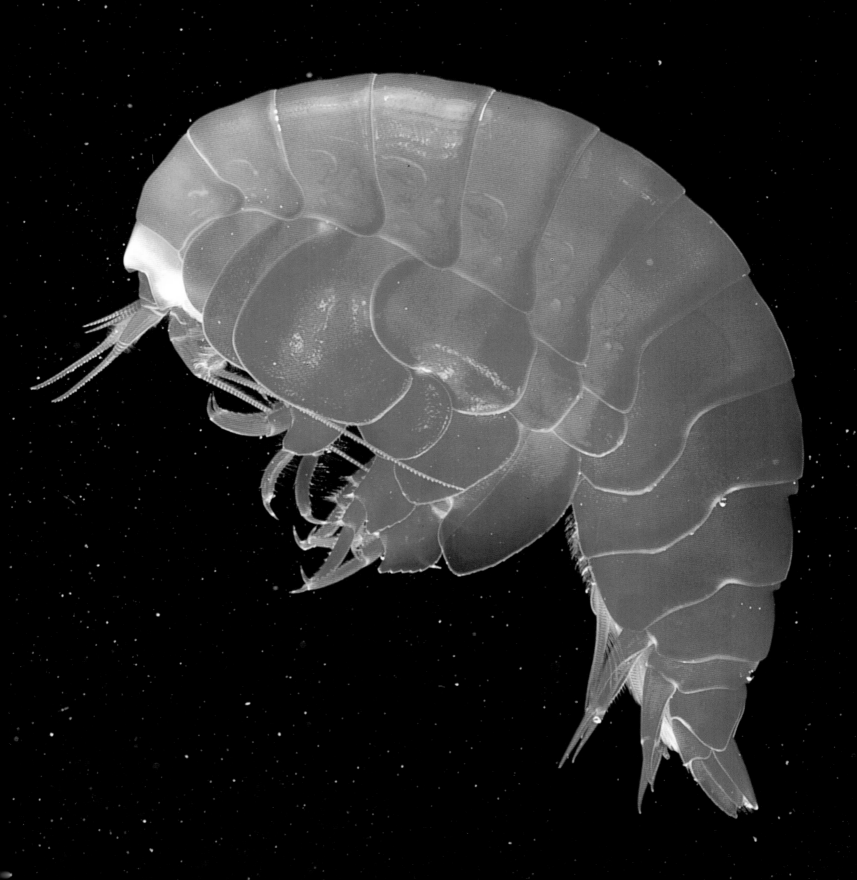

150

150 THE GIANT'S CAUSEWAY,
COUNTY ANTRIM, NORTHERN
IRELAND
(Heather Angel)
REGULAR GEOMETRIC LAVA
FORMATIONS OCCUR WHEN GREAT
THICKNESSES OF MOLTEN BASALT
FROM A VOLCANIC ERUPTION COOL
VERY SLOWLY. THE GIANT'S
CAUSEWAY CONSISTS OF
THOUSANDS OF COLUMNS, MOST
OF THEM HEXAGONAL, FORMING A
STAIRCASE DOWN TO THE SEA.

151

151 A HYDROTHERMAL VENT,
GALAPAGOS RIFT, PACIFIC OCEAN
(Robert Hessler/Planet Earth)
DEEP DOWN ON THE OCEAN FLOOR
AT THE CREST OF THE MID-OCEAN
RIDGE, FISSURES IN THE EARTH'S
CRUST ALLOW THE SEA-WATER TO
CIRCULATE AND TO HEAT UP. THE
HOT WATER THAT EMERGES FROM
THE SEA FLOOR, FORCED UP BY
CONVECTION, IS LADEN WITH
CHEMICALS THAT PRECIPITATE AS
BLACK PARTICLES. THESE 'BLACK
SMOKERS', OR HYDROTHERMAL
VENTS, SUPPORT AN ENTIRE MINI-
ECOSYSTEM TEEMING WITH CRABS,
TUBE WORMS, MOLLUSCS AND
MORE – WHICH FLY IN THE FACE OF
NATURE, DEPENDING ON
CHEMICALS FOR LIFE RATHER
THAN SUNLIGHT.

152

152 KILAUEA VOLCANO, HAWAII
(Bob Cranston/Norbert Wu Photography)
THE HAWAIIAN CHAIN CONSISTS OF A SERIES OF VOLCANIC ISLANDS FORMED AS
THE EARTH'S CRUST BENEATH THE PACIFIC OCEAN MOVES NORTHWESTWARD
OVER AN ABNORMALLY HOT ZONE IN THE EARTH'S UPPER MANTLE, AND LIQUID
MAGMA IS FORCED UP THROUGH IT. KILAUEA VOLCANO, ON THE ISLAND OF
HAWAII AT THE SOUTHEAST END OF THE CHAIN, IS THE YOUNGEST AND ONE OF
THE MOST ACTIVE VOLCANOES IN THE WORLD.

153

154

153 and 155   STAIR HOLE, DORSET
(Heather Angel), AND CLIFFS,
CORNWALL (Heather Angel)
TECTONIC PLATE MOVEMENT AND
VOLCANIC ACTIVITY MAKE THE
EARTH'S CRUST EXPAND AND
SPREAD, THRUSTING SOME PARTS
OF IT UP ABOVE THE SEA OR BACK
DOWN INTO THE EARTH'S
INTERIOR. THE ACUTE FOLDING
SEEN IN STAIR HOLE IS THE RESULT
OF SUCH PRESSURE. LAYERS OF
ROCK THAT ONCE FORMED THE
OCEAN FLOOR CAN BE SEEN
DEFORMED AND NOW EXPOSED.
THE CORNISH CLIFFS, SEEN HERE,
SHOW A SIMILAR FOLDING.

154   SANDFLATS, NORTH UIST,
SCOTLAND
(Laurie Campbell)
FLATS OF MUD OR SAND FORM
ALONGSIDE MOST OF THE
ESTUARIES OF THE WORLD, THEIR
AREAS EXTENDING OR
DIMINISHING ACCORDING TO THE
TIDES. SEDIMENT BORNE BY RIVERS
EMPTIES INTO THE SEAS'
ESTUARINE BASINS; THE TIDE THEN
RETURNS SOME OF THESE
DEPOSITS TO THE LAND, FORMING
SANDFLATS.

155

156

156 and 157 WARREN POINT, DEVON (David Noton)**, AND POINT OF STOER,
SUTHERLAND, SCOTLAND** (David Noton)
THE VARIOUS MINERAL STRUCTURES OF ROCKS DETERMINE COASTLINE
FORMATIONS. AFTER MILLIONS OF YEARS OF WEATHERING BY SEA AND WIND,
ONLY THE MORE RESISTANT SUBSTANCES REMAIN. GRANITE AND CERTAIN
LIMESTONES YIELD ONLY SLOWLY, BUT THE SEA UNDERCUTS EVEN THESE,
CARVING OUT STACKS AND CAVES, ARCHES AND CLIFFS. WITH THE RELENTLESS
POUNDING OF THE WAVES, SOFTER ROCKS CRUMBLE AWAY, AND THE DEBRIS IS
WASHED ALONG THE COAST TO CREATE BEACHES AND PEBBLE BANKS.

158

158, 159 and 160 **SEABIRDS ON ROUGH SEAS, AUCKLAND ISLAND, NEW ZEALAND**
(Kim Westerskov), **ISLAY, SCOTLAND** (Laurie Campbell), **AND BIG SISTER ISLAND,**
NEW ZEALAND (Kim Westerskov/OSF)
DRAMATIC CLIFFS ARE FORMED WHERE ROUGH SEAS, CAUSED BY DISTANT AS
WELL AS LOCAL STORMS, POUND AT THE BASE. THE WAVES CARRY AWAY LOOSE
OR WEAKENED ROCK, AND HURL FRAGMENTS AGAINST THE FACE. WAVES CAN
EVEN COMPRESS AIR INTO THE ROCKS' JOINTS, SO THAT WHEN THEY RETREAT
THE AIR EXPLODES. STORM WAVES EXERT PRESSURE UP TO 30 TONNES PER
SQUARE METRE – ENOUGH TO DEFEAT THE MOST RESILIENT ROCKS.

159

160

161

161 AN ATOLL FORMING: HERON ISLAND, GREAT BARRIER REEF, QUEENSLAND

(Gerry Ellis)

AN ATOLL IS A CORAL REEF IN THE SHAPE OF A RING OR A HORSESHOE,
ENCLOSING A LAGOON. ACCORDING TO DARWIN, AN ATOLL BEGINS TO FORM
WHEN A CORAL FRINGE GROWS AROUND A VOLCANIC ISLAND. THE LOAD WHICH
THE VOLCANO IMPOSES ON THE EARTH'S CRUST MAKES IT BEND UNDER THE
WEIGHT, AND SO THE ISLAND BEGINS TO SINK. THE CORAL, THOUGH, GROWS
FASTER THAN THE ISLAND SINKS, RESULTING IN A CORAL RING SURROUNDING A
LAGOON. MOST ATOLLS ARE FOUND IN THE PACIFIC OCEAN. THEY FORM THE
ISLAND SYSTEM OF MICRONESIA, IN THE INDIAN OCEAN, THE MALDIVES AND THE
LACCADIVES. ATOLLS MAY RANGE IN SIZE FROM LESS THAN A KILOMETRE TO
OVER 120 KM (75 MILES) IN DIAMETER, AND ARE VERY LOW-LYING. BECAUSE OF
THIS, EVEN SMALL RISES IN SEA LEVEL MAKE THEM VERY VULNERABLE TO
FLOODING.

162 THE BEACH BELOW MOUNT SANTUBONG, SARAWAK

(Heather Angel)

WASHED DOWN FROM THE LAND BY RIVERS, ERODED SEDIMENT ACCUMULATES
IN THE COASTAL ZONE – SEEN HERE AS THE DARKER WAVY BANDS ALONG THE
TIDEMARK. THIS PROCESS IS THE SOURCE OF MANY OF THE MINERALS FOUND
DISSOLVED IN SEA-WATER. THE LARGER GRAINS OF SEDIMENT FIND THEIR WAY
INTO THE DEEP OCEAN BASINS, FORMING THE MASSIVE ACCUMULATIONS OF
SEDIMENT AT THE FOOT OF THE CONTINENTAL SLOPE.

164

163 CORAL ISLANDS, PALAU, MICRONESIA
(David Hall)
WHEN ISLANDS ARE FORMED, THE FIRST LIFE TO COLONIZE THE NEW LAND
IS NOT ALWAYS PLANTS. FIRST MAY COME INSECTS AND SMALL ORGANISMS
THAT FEED ON CARRION WASHED UP ON THE SHORE. BOTH PLANTS AND
ANIMAL ORGANISMS ARE OFTEN FIRST BROUGHT BY SEABIRDS.

164 A CORAL LAGOON, FIJI
(Norbert Wu)
LAGOONS ARE WARM, SHALLOW, QUIET WATERWAYS SEPARATED FROM THE
OPEN SEA BY SANDBARS, BARRIER ISLANDS OR CORAL REEFS, OR A
COMBINATION OF THESE. CORAL ATOLLS ENCLOSE ROUGHLY CIRCULAR
LAGOONS, WHICH THEMSELVES ARE ALSO CORAL-BOTTOMED, LIKE THE ONE
SHOWN HERE. THE PALM TREES FRINGING THE LAGOON ARE TYPICAL CORAL
ISLAND VEGETATION.

168

167 and 169   A CHINSTRAP PENGUIN CHICK HATCHES (Ben Osborne), **AND AN EMPEROR CHICK NESTLES ON ITS PARENT'S FEET** (Kim Westerskov) FEMALE PENGUINS LAY THEIR SINGLE WHITE EGGS IN MAY OR JUNE. FOR THE WHOLE OF THE SIXTY DAYS' INCUBATION, DURING THE COLDEST PART OF THE ANTARCTIC WINTER, THE MALE EMPEROR STANDS WITH HIS EGG ON HIS FEET, TUCKED UNDER A FATTY FOLD OF SKIN TO KEEP IT WARM. THE FEMALE, WHICH HAS BEEN AWAY FEEDING AT SEA, RETURNS ON HATCHING DAY, THEN FEEDS THE CHICK. NOW CARE ROLES ARE REVERSED, AND THE MALE GOES OFF IN SEARCH OF THE OPEN SEA AND A SQUARE MEAL.

168   KING PENGUINS, WITH CHICKS (Gerry Ellis) THE BROWN, FLUFFY FLEDGLINGS ARE ONE YEAR OLD – PENNED IN BY THE ADULTS IN THIS WAY, THEY ARE LESS VULNERABLE TO PREDATORS. COLONIES USUALLY NUMBER 20,000-60,000 BIRDS. KING PENGUIN CHICKS MATURE FOR A FULL YEAR ON LAND – LONGER THAN ANY OTHER SPECIES – FEEDING ON KRILL REGURGITATED BY THEIR PARENTS, BEFORE THEY GO TO SEA FOR THE FIRST TIME.

169

170   ROYAL ALBATROSSES NESTING, MIDDLE SISTER ISLAND
(Kim Westerskov)
ALBATROSSES SPEND MANY MONTHS ON THE COLD SOUTHERN SEA, COMING ASHORE ONLY TO BREED, USUALLY ON WINDSWEPT ISLANDS FAR FROM HUMAN HABITATION. ROYAL ALBATROSSES BREED EVERY TWO YEARS, AND THE EGG TAKES UP TO THREE MONTHS TO INCUBATE. ONCE HATCHED, THE CHICK MAY STAY IN THE NEST FOR A YEAR.

171

172

**171 and 172   A GANNET COLONY,
BRITAIN** (Richard Matthews/Planet Earth),
**AND BLUE-EYED SHAGS WITH
THEIR CHICKS, ANTARCTICA** (Ben
Osborne)
THE NORTHERN GANNET LIVES IN
LARGE, NOISY COLONIES ALONG
COASTS, AND FORAGES IN THE SEA,
MAKING FREQUENT COMPLEX
DISPLAYS TO DO WITH PAIR-
BONDING AND SITE OWNERSHIP. AT
NESTING TIME GANNETS ARE AT
THEIR MOST AGGRESSIVE. IF AN
ADULT BIRD LANDS AT THE WRONG
NEST, OR IF A CHICK STRAYS INTO
ANOTHER'S TERRITORY, THE
OFFENDER MAY BE PECKED TO
DEATH. SHAGS, TOO, ARE
VIGOROUS IN DEFENCE OF THEIR
NESTS AND YOUNG.

173   A KITTIWAKE AT ITS NEST
(Laurie Campbell)
KITTIWAKES CONGREGATE IN
LARGE COLONIES ON NARROW
CLIFF EDGES AND GULLIES. THEY
SECURE THEIR NESTS WITH
SEAWEED, WHICH ADHERES TO THE
ROCK AS IT DRIES. ABOUT HALF A
MILLION PAIRS BREED IN BRITAIN
AND IRELAND. ONCE SLAUGHTERED
FOR SPORT AND TO PROVIDE
FEATHERS FOR WOMEN'S HATS, THE
KITTIWAKE IS NOW A PROTECTED
SPECIES.

173

174

174   TWO GIANT SPINED STARFISH, POINT LOBOS, MONTEREY, CALIFORNIA
(Norbert Wu)

THE INTERTIDAL ZONE OF TEMPERATE COASTS IS OFTEN HOST TO STARFISH LIKE
THESE GIANTS, WELL ADAPTED TO THE RIGOURS OF EXPOSURE WHEN THE TIDE
IS OUT, AS IT IS HERE. MOST STARFISH HAVE FIVE ARMS, BUT SOME SPECIES HAVE
UP TO TWENTY-FIVE. EACH ARM CONTAINS AN EXTENSION OF THE BODY CAVITY
AND ORGANS. THE NUMEROUS PLATES UNDER THE SKIN, WHICH FORM THE
EXOSKELETON, ARE LINKED BY MUSCLE AND CONNECTIVE TISSUE, GIVING THE
APPARENTLY RIGID CREATURE CONSIDERABLE FLEXIBILITY. STARFISH AND MANY
OTHER ANIMALS TAKE REFUGE AMONGST THE WET POOLS AND TRAILING WEEDS
WHICH ARE ALSO CHARACTERISTIC OF THE INTERTIDAL ZONE.

175   SURF GRASS, TORREY PINES STATE PARK, CALIFORNIA, AT LOW TIDE
(Richard Herrmann)
MANY COASTAL SEAWEEDS ARE EXPOSED AT LOW TIDE, PROVIDING A
COMFORTABLY WET SHELTER FOR SMALL ANIMALS SUCH AS SHELLFISH, WHICH
MIGHT OTHERWISE DIE FROM DESICCATION. ON THE SANDY SEA FLOORS OFF THE
WEST COAST OF AMERICA, AND IN THE CARIBBEAN, GRASSES PROLIFERATE.
SUBMERGED AT HIGH TIDE, THEY RESEMBLE UNDERWATER MEADOWS. AND, LIKE
THEIR TERRESTRIAL COUNTERPARTS, THEY ARE SOMETIMES OVER-GRAZED BY
THE CREATURES THAT FEED ON THEM. SEA URCHINS, FOR INSTANCE, OFTEN
NIBBLE SO CLOSE TO THE ROOTS THAT THE PLANTS DIE OFF. BUT ALGAE MAY
SPRING UP ON PATCHES OF BARE SAND, AND IN TIME THE GRASSES RETURN.

176

177

178

176 and 177 SEA URCHINS (Richard Herrmann),
PISASTER STARFISH AND ANEMONES (Richard Herrmann), **CALIFORNIA**
THE INTERTIDAL ZONE, WHERE THESE CREATURES ARE FOUND, IS THE PART OF
THE SHORE THAT IS UNDER WATER AT HIGH TIDE AND EXPOSED WHEN THE TIDE
IS LOW; IT OFTEN SUPPORTS HIGHLY SPECIALIZED COMMUNITIES OF PLANTS AND
ANIMALS, GEARED TO ENDURE THE HARSH CONDITIONS BROUGHT ABOUT BY
WIND AND WAVE.

178 GIANT STARFISH FEEDING ON MUSSELS, INTERTIDAL ZONE, CALIFORNIA
(Richard Herrmann)
USING ITS STICKY TUBE FEET, THE CARNIVOROUS STARFISH PRISES OPEN THE
SHELLS OF PREY SUCH AS MUSSELS. STARFISH HAVE NO TEETH. SOME ENGULF
THEIR FOOD, WHILE OTHERS EVERT THEIR STOMACHS ON TO A MEAL: THEY
SECRETE DIGESTIVE ENZYMES OVER THE PREY, WHICH THEY THEN SUCK BACK
INTO THEIR BODIES ALONG WITH THEIR STOMACHS.

179

180

181

179 and 180   BLADDER-WRACK (Mark Mattock/Planet Earth),
AND CHANNEL-WRACK (Laurie Campbell), **BRITAIN**
FOUND IN THE MID-SHORE REGION OF ROCKY COASTLINES, AT LOW TIDE THESE
FLATTENED, FORKING SEAWEEDS PROVIDE SHELTER UNDER THEIR DAMP
BLANKET FOR ANIMALS SUCH AS WINKLES AND ANEMONES.

181   KELP, ORKNEYS, SCOTLAND
(Mark Mattock/Planet Earth)
BESIDES FURNISHING A HABITAT FOR MARINE CREATURES, MANY KELPS HAVE
LONG BEEN OF COMMERCIAL INTEREST. THE OLD KELP-BURNING INDUSTRY USED
CERTAIN SPECIES IN THE PRODUCTION OF SODA, POTASH AND IODINE, AND SOME
ARE USED NOW AS A SOURCE OF ALGINIC ACID, WHICH IS IMPORTANT AS AN
EMULSIFYING AGENT.

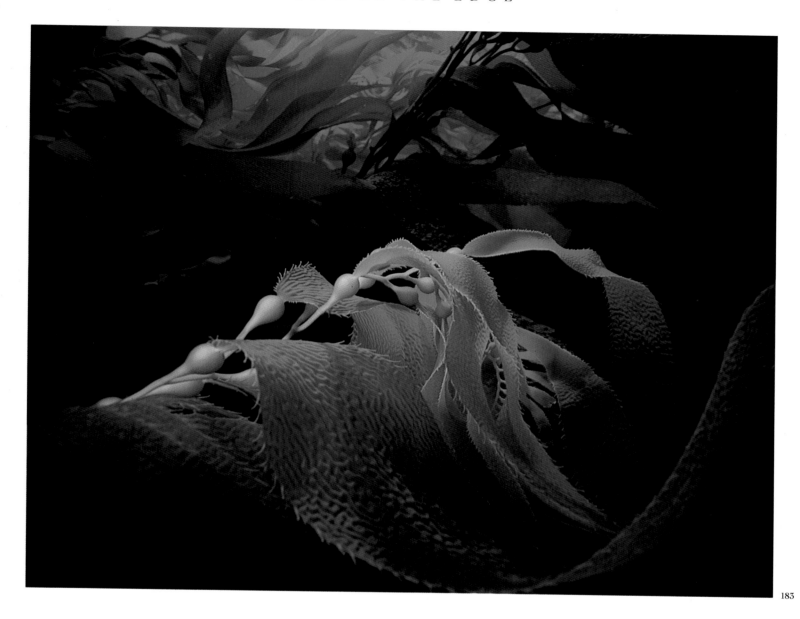

183

182 and 183 A KELP HOLDFAST, IRELAND (John Lythgoe/Planet Earth),
AND A GIANT KELP BLADE, CALIFORNIA (Georgette Douwma/Planet Earth)
THESE LARGE SEAWEEDS OFTEN GROW EXTENSIVELY IN TEMPERATE COASTAL
WATERS, SOMETIMES RESEMBLING ELABORATELY BRANCHED MATS OR LACY
FANS. KELPS HAVE NO ROOTS, BUT ANCHOR THEMSELVES TO THE SEA FLOOR
WITH 'HOLDFASTS', WHICH HELP THEM TO ENDURE ROUGH SEAS. *MACROCYSTIS
PYRIFERA*, THE LARGEST OF THE GIANT KELPS, HAS AT THE BASE OF EACH LEAF-
LIKE BLADE AN AIR BLADDER WHICH MAKES IT BUOYANT IN THE WATER.
SUPPORTED BY THE BLADDERS, THE BLADES FLOAT ON THE WATER'S SURFACE: A
SINGLE FROND MAY BE 60 METRES (200 FT) LONG.

184

184   A SOUTHERN BULL ELEPHANT SEAL, SOUTH ISLAND, NEW ZEALAND

(Donna Kelly)

THE LARGEST OF THE PINNIPEDS, MALE ELEPHANT SEALS OFTEN REACH A
LENGTH OF 5.5 METRES (18 FT) AND WEIGH 2,300 KG (5,000 LB). THEY ARE SOME OF
THE MANY ANIMALS THAT OCCASIONALLY USE FISH-RICH KELP FORESTS AS
HUNTING GROUNDS. ELEPHANT SEALS ARE TRUE SEALS, CLASSED AS SUCH
BECAUSE, UNLIKE FUR SEALS AND SEA LIONS, THEY POSSESS A THICK LAYER OF
BLUBBER AND ARE PROPELLED MAINLY BY THEIR HIND FLIPPERS. THEIR USUALLY
FLOPPY SNOUTS – WHICH GIVE THEM THEIR NAME – FILL WITH AIR WHEN THEY
ARE EXCITED OR ANGRY, PRODUCING A DEEP ROAR WHEN THE AIR IS RELEASED.
DURING THE MATING SEASON THE MALES FIGHT PROLONGED AND BLOODY
BATTLES WITH EACH OTHER. ELEPHANT SEALS USUALLY SLEEP ON THE SHORE
DURING THE DAY, AND FEED AT NIGHT. THE SOUTHERN SPECIES CAN BE FOUND
IN ALL PARTS OF THE WORLD, BUT IS PARTICULARLY WIDESPREAD ON SUB-
ANTARCTIC ISLANDS.

185   A GREY WHALE IN A KELP FOREST, OFF THE COAST OF CALIFORNIA

(Howard Hall/Planet Earth)

GREY WHALES MAKE THE LONGEST KNOWN ANNUAL MIGRATION OF ANY
MAMMAL, JOURNEYING UP TO 11,000 KM (7,000 MILES) FROM THEIR SUMMER
FEEDING GROUNDS IN THE ARCTIC AND ANTARCTIC, TO WINTER IN THE BAYS AND
LAGOONS OF TROPICAL COASTAL WATERS, WHERE THEY BREED AND RAISE THEIR
CALVES. THOUGH THEY LIVE MAINLY OFF THEIR BLUBBER DURING THE LONG
MONTHS OF MIGRATION AND BREEDING, THEY WILL OCCASIONALLY BROWSE
AMONG THE KELP FORESTS NEAR THEIR CALVING BAYS; THEY DO NOT EAT THE
SEAWEED ITSELF, BUT INSTEAD GRAZE ON THE THOUSANDS OF MICRO-
ORGANISMS WHICH INHABIT THE KELP BLADES. GREY WHALES ALSO EAT
AMPHIPOD SHRIMPS, WHICH THEY FIND NEAR OR ON THE SEA FLOOR. THEY
APPEAR TO USE THEIR SNOUTS TO STIR UP THE SEDIMENT, AND THEN FILTER THE
DISTURBED ORGANISM-RICH WATER.

186

186 and 187 DAMSELFISH OVER TABLE CORAL, FIJI (B. Jones & M. Shimlock),
AND LION-FISH, SOLOMON ISLANDS (B. Jones & M. Shimlock)
THE SPECTACULAR LIFE OF THE CORAL REEFS: USUALLY OCCURRING IN
LARGE GROUPS ABOVE CORAL HEADS, DAMSELFISH MAINLY EAT PLANKTON,
BUT OCCASIONALLY THEY FEED ON THE ALGAE THAT GROW ON THE CORAL,
INTO WHICH THEY RETREAT AT THE FIRST SIGN OF DANGER. THEY NEVER
STRAY FAR FROM THEIR CHOSEN HOME, IN THIS CASE AN *ACROPORA* CORAL.
THE LION-FISH SHOWN HERE LIVE IN THE HOLES AT THE BASE OF THE RED
SEA-FAN. LIKE ALL OF THE SCORPION-FISH FAMILY, OF WHICH THE LION-
FISH IS A MEMBER, IT HAS VENOMOUS SPINES. DURING THE DAY IT MAY
HIDE IN REEF CREVICES, BECOMING ACTIVE AT NIGHT.

189 A YELLOW-CROWNED NIGHT HERON PREENING IN A MANGROVE, SANIBEL ISLAND, FLORIDA
(J. Brian Alker/Planet Earth)
MANY BIRDS ROOST IN MANGROVES, SUCH AS EGRETS AND THE MAINLY NOCTURNAL YELLOW-CROWNED NIGHT HERON. THE MANGROVE SWAMPS OFFER A RICH HUNTING GROUND FOR THE FISH AND CRUSTACEANS ON WHICH THE BIRDS FEED.

188 MANGROVES, BELIZE
(Jim Clare/Partridge Films/OSF)
MANGROVES ARE COASTAL FORESTS THAT GROW IN SALT MARSHES AND TIDAL ESTUARIES, INUNDATED WITH FRESH OR SALT WATER, DEPENDING ON THE TIDE. THE TREES ARE CHARACTERIZED BY WOODY TANGLES OF ROOTS, WHICH MAY BE SUBMERGED FOR LONG INTERVALS; THESE PRODUCE OFFSHOOTS PROJECTING SEVERAL FEET AWAY FROM THE PARENT, WHICH CREATE NEW TREES. SEDIMENT ACCUMULATES UNDER THE MANGROVES' ROOTS.

190 MUDSKIPPERS IN A MANGROVE, SOUTH EAST ASIA
(Zig Leszczynski/OSF)
MANGROVE SPECIALISTS, THESE SMALL PREDATORS – ONLY ABOUT 8 CM (3 IN) LONG – ARE EXTREMELY AGGRESSIVE WHEN PURSUING PREY, WHICH INCLUDES SPIDERS, INSECTS, WORMS AND MOLLUSCS. THE PROTRUDING EYE PROVIDES A WIDE-ANGLE VIEW WHEN THE MUDSKIPPER IS SUBMERGED UNDER WATER OR SUNK IN MUD.

CHAPTER TEN

THE HUMAN OCEANS:
PROTECTORS AND PLUNDERERS
PROFESSOR ALASTAIR COUPER

As far back as we can look in the history of human settlement, people have lived close to the sea, and gathered food and other vital resources from its waters. Certainly, prehistoric peoples were gathering fish, crustaceans and molluscs from around the Great Barrier Reef and Papua New Guinea by 25,000 BC. Others ventured very early across the oceans in search of new homelands; well before 1,500 BC, whole communities pushed out from the island region of southeast Asia into the Pacific.

THOUSANDS OF YEARS BEFORE IT WAS 'DISCOVERED' BY Westerners, Polynesian seafarers explored the entire Pacific Ocean – easily the largest feature on the planet, covering one third of its surface – and colonized its many islands. These societies had no mechanical timepieces nor metal tools, but they built fine ships, and possessed a sophisticated understanding of ocean navigation and marine ecology: the knowledge of a culture shaped by the sea.

On the coasts, atolls and islands of the world there are still a few communities who depend on the ocean for survival, people who understand its rhythms and ecology on far more levels than do many modern scientists. On the tiny coral islets of Faraulek, Ifalik and others outlying the Yap island system in Micronesia, people live much as they have done for centuries, benefiting from a treasury of traditional knowledge accumulated over many generations.

So various and complex are the ecosystems of coral reefs that they are still mysterious to most professionals, yet the Yap islanders are accomplished reef ecologists, who exploit their knowledge in precise and sometimes unexpected ways. Travelling the reef flats in small wooden outrigger canoes, they trail

191   A BOY WITH A SHELL, IFALIK, YAP ISLANDS, MICRONESIA

(B. & C. Alexander)

FROM THE EARLIEST TIMES, PEOPLE HAVE LIVED CLOSE TO THE SEA AND HARVESTED FOOD FROM ITS WATERS. BUT, UNDERSTANDING THEIR DEPENDENCE ON THE ENVIRONMENT, THEY HAVE ALSO BEEN CAREFUL TO CONSERVE IT.

baited lines, or dive down with bamboo harpoons to hunt among the coral for lobsters, giant clams, octopus, sea urchins, parrotfish, surgeonfish, goatfish and snappers, and many less familiar animals – some still unnamed by science. Besides food, this bounty is used to make ornaments and tools, while medicines and fishing poisons are manufactured from the very toxins that many reef creatures produce for defence.

Further out at sea in their sailing canoes, Pacific islanders catch large fish such as yellowfin tuna and deep-sea grouper, and even trap dolphins and sharks. Skilled boat-builders and voyagers, they are able to navigate open ocean using only the sun, the waves and stars as guides. Equally subtle signs assist their hunting: schooling animals are located by the behaviour of birds, or the murmur of fish beneath the water; accurate predictions are made according to the phases of the moon, wind direction, currents, and the mood of the sea itself.

Half-way across the world, along the icy sea margins of northwest Greenland and Canada's North West Territories, there are Inuit groups who still live much of the year as hunter gatherers. Large mammals proliferate here, and besides fish the people hunt narwhal and beluga whales, polar bear, walrus, fox and caribou; but the staple diet of coastal Inuit is seal, especially ringed seal – the commonest Arctic species.

Hunting techniques vary with the seasons. During the short polar summer when the sea ice thaws, some hunt whales with harpoons from kayaks. When the sea has frozen over again, they may travel enormous distances by dog sled, or more latterly snowmobile, in search of game. Even otherwise sedentary Inuit make brief expeditions, but some families spend weeks, even months, travelling the ice, occasionally building as they go the temporary shelters which Westerners know as igloos. With a frugality typical of a subsistence lifestyle, the Inuit waste nothing of a kill: excess meat is instantly frozen, or dried; seal fat, a vital source of vitamins and energy, may be stored; sinews become twine and skins become furs, essential protection against the bitter Arctic weather.

But the relationship which the Pacific Islanders, the Inuit and others have with their environment does more than merely inform their hunting techniques. Because they understand the marine ecosystem, they also perceive its vulnerability. Since they are aware that their own survival, and that of future generations, depend upon the welfare of the sea and its inhabitants, they are careful to use its resources in a sustainable, non-destructive way.

In the Pacific Islands, for example, people grasped very early that reef and lagoon resources were finite. Before Samoa fell foul of colonization and industrialization, a complex system of traditional rights, with reef ownership vested from generation to generation in the village chiefs, worked to ensure that the reefs were protected. A similar system is used by indigenous cultures throughout the Coral Islands, Papua New Guinea and elsewhere. In fact, many societies have adopted the strategy of allocating certain stretches of water to particular communities: individuals with a responsibility to their own close-knit group have strong incentives not to over-fish.

Other rules are more specific. In parts of Fiji it is forbidden to take small fish, on the grounds that these are the food of larger fish. Many societies protect certain species during their vulnerable periods – for instance, by closing hunting during spawning time. In the East Sepik region of Papua New Guinea, turtles may not be eaten during certain seasons; elsewhere, dugongs can be consumed only on festive occasions.

Such practices are reinforced by something deeper than economics. They have at their root a reverence for nature which is inherent in traditional societies the world over. In West Africa, shrines are dedicated to sea gods; in Papua New Guinea, complex propitiation rituals take place after a shark capture. The Yap islanders celebrate a dolphin catch with a ceremony of dancing and singing, while the Inuit maintain that every living organism possesses a spirit, which will yield itself willingly to the hunter if treated with proper respect. This means, among other things, no indulging in mass slaughter, even if the animals are many – even when the hunter has a gun, as many Inuit now do. Old taboos have it that only five foxes may be taken on any one hunt. And if too many seals are killed in one place, they will return as humans in boats of ice to take revenge.

Thus rules, values and beliefs forbid over-exploitation, an ethic that has enabled ocean peoples to make a living from the sea for thousands of years. But today, guns have become widespread and missionaries still discourage as pagan a spiritual respect for nature. Many indigenous groups are losing their knowledge and abandoning sustainable hunting practices; settlers are introducing alien values and economies in their place, assaulting traditional cultures at every level. But the greatest threat to the ocean peoples' way of life is the destruction of the marine environment itself.

The logic of protecting the habitat and animals on which you depend seems simple, but it has eluded many more technically advanced cultures, who over the last few hundred years have tended to regard the sea as a free-for-all hunting ground. Indeed the idea of renewable resources is foreign to industrial and high-technology societies that depend on innovation.

Today, the consequences are painfully clear. Creatures such as the great auk and Stellar's sea cow are extinct. Numerous species of fur seal, sea otter, dolphin, great whale, turtle and dugong are endangered, while stocks of many commercial fish – for instance, the bluefin tuna and Newfoundland cod – have fallen to dangerously low levels. Meanwhile, sewage, industrial and radioactive wastes spilling from the coast, or dumped at sea by accident or design, have poisoned the waters of many areas.

There are currently few conservational rules being implemented governing the use of the sea – whether for transport, tourism, waste disposal, energy production, mineral extraction, or commercial fishing – though all these can, and frequently do, damage marine ecosystems. Since 1982, countries have had sovereignty over 320-km (200-mile) Exclusive Economic Zones extending from their coasts, but most have not yet begun to use sustainably the resources within them. This bodes ill for the future, especially now that new mineral, oil and natural gas resources have been discovered beneath the sea, and technological advances may soon enable them to be extracted.

Growing populations will put further pressure on the overstretched oceans. Already, 70 per cent of people live on or near the coasts. Given that within sixty or seventy years, world populations are likely to rise from the current five billion to around twelve billion, the demands made on the sea will be greater than ever before.

If we are to meet the complex challenges of the future, long-term planning must replace short-sighted exploitation; technological progress must be combined with sustainable use of the sea's resources. Approaches could include marine agriculture, energy production, even mining; much is possible, providing the limitations of the environment and balance of the ecosystem are taken into account.

In a gradual move towards protecting and conserving the whole marine environment as distinct from individual species, some countries are introducing measures such as fishing-gear restrictions, prohibited fishing areas, and closed seasons during spawning. Such practices are familiar to ocean peoples. Indeed, it has been argued that all the conservation methods which Western societies are only now considering have been employed by island societies for centuries.

We can no longer afford to underestimate the knowledge and understanding of ocean peoples. Neither should we continue to undervalue the importance of their deep-held respect for the oceans, which contrasts sharply with the 'land-mindedness' even of governments whose countries are surrounded by sea. Consider the Indonesian word *tanahair*, which translates as 'homeland', but literally means 'homelandwater'. Here lies the crux. The people of the oceans do not regard land as the centre of the universe, the seas merely as a convenient dumping ground and resource to be plundered. They know that both are necessary parts of a greater whole.

---

192 A REEF FISHERMAN WITH HIS CATCH, YAP, MICRONESIA

(B. & C. Alexander)

FISHERMEN OF THE CORAL ISLANDS OF YAP DIVE FOR FISH ON THE REEFS BY NIGHT, EQUIPPED WITH JUST A SPEAR, A TORCH AND A MASK. THE FISH ARE ATTRACTED BY THE LIGHT, AND HAULS ARE OFTEN RICH. LOCAL MARTIN LUGWAN DISPLAYS HIS NIGHT'S CATCH OF LOBSTER AND FISH.

194

193   LABUAN HADJI VILLAGE, BORNEO
(B. Jones and M. Shimlock)

MUCH OF THE COASTAL FRINGE OF BORNEO IS LOW-LYING AND SWAMPY. LABUAN
HADJI IS ONE OF THE OLDEST 'WATER VILLAGES' IN THE AREA; MOST CHILDREN
LEARN TO SWIM AND PADDLE A CANOE BEFORE THEY CAN WALK. THE PEOPLE
HAVE A LONG TRADITION OF LIVING VERY CLOSE TO THE SEA. NEARLY EVERYONE
MAKES THEIR LIVELIHOOD FROM IT, AND MOST STILL USE TRADITIONAL SAILING
CRAFT TO FISH FROM. MANY HOUSES HAVE NETS SLUNG BETWEEN THEM FOR
TRAPPING BAIT, WHICH IS LATER USED FOR FISHING.

194   A FISHING AND BOAT-BUILDING VILLAGE, BONE RATE, INDONESIA
(David Hall)

IN THIS SMALL VILLAGE IN THE BONE RATE GROUP OF ISLANDS IN CENTRAL
INDONESIA, THE MAIN LIVELIHOODS ARE BOAT-BUILDING AND FISHING. AS WELL
AS BEING FISHING VESSELS, THE BOATS ARE USED FOR TRANSPORT BETWEEN
ISLANDS. THE COUNTRY CONSISTS OF 13,677 ISLANDS, STRETCHING IN A CRESCENT
FOR MORE THAN 5,000 KM (3,200 MILES), FROM THE INDIAN OCEAN TO THE
PACIFIC. SIX THOUSAND OF THE ISLANDS ARE INHABITED; IN 1890 FOSSILS OF
JAVA MAN (*HOMO ERECTUS*) WERE FOUND HERE, DATING BACK 500,000 YEARS.

195

195 and 196   CHINESE FISHING NETS AT COCHIN, ON THE ARABIAN SEA, INDIA
(Colin Caket/Zefa), **AND MOZAMBIQUAN FISHERMEN**
DRAGGING IN THEIR CATCH (V. Wentzel/Zefa)
AMONG BOTH TRADITIONAL AND INDUSTRIALIZED FISHERMEN, NETS STILL
CONSTITUTE, ALL OVER THE WORLD, THE MOST POPULAR MEANS OF GATHERING
THE SEAS' HARVEST. CANTILEVER FISHING NETS (195) ARE AN ANCIENT IMPORT
FROM CHINA. THE FISHERMEN SHOWN OPPOSITE, ON THE COAST OF
MOZAMBIQUE NEAR WHERE THE ZAMBEZI RIVER FLOWS INTO THE INDIAN
OCEAN, ARE HAULING IN THEIR CATCH IN A NET SET SOME TIME PREVIOUSLY.

197   STILT FISHING, GALLE, SRI LANKA
(Heather Angel)
STILT FISHING IS ANOTHER ANCIENT AND EXTREMELY SIMPLE BUT EFFICIENT
TECHNIQUE USED BY MANY COASTAL COMMUNITIES. THE STILTS ARE PLACED AT
FIXED SITES, ALLOWING FISHING IN DEEPER WATER, WHERE FISH ARE OFTEN
LARGER AND MORE PLENTIFUL.

196

197

198   DRYING A SQUID, MADAGASCAR

(Frans Lanting/Zefa)

IN HOT REGIONS, DRYING IS THE STANDARD WAY OF PRESERVING FISH,
THOUGH IT IS OFTEN ALSO SALTED. THROUGH MUCH OF SOUTH EAST ASIA,
EAST AFRICA AND THE MEDITERRANEAN, SQUID HAS LONG BEEN A STAPLE;
IT IS ONLY RECENTLY THAT IT HAS BECOME A COMMERCIAL SPECIES IN THE
USA AND OTHER PARTS OF EUROPE. THIS VEZO FISHERMAN, BELONGING TO
A FISHING COMMUNITY IN THE SOUTH OF MADAGASCAR, USES TIME-
HONOURED METHODS TO MAKE HIS LIVELIHOOD; HIS MOST ESSENTIAL
ASSET IS HIS OUTRIGGER CANOE. FISHING IN MADAGASCAR TAKES PLACE
LARGELY IN COASTAL LAGOONS.

199

199, 200 and 201   MUSSEL-HARVESTING AT SCARDOVARI, ITALY (Zefa),
A SOUTH EAST ASIAN FISHERMAN (Holdsworth/Zefa) AND AN INUIT FISHERMAN
WITH A HARPOON, GREENLAND (B. & C. Alexander)
SMALL POPULATIONS AND NON-MECHANIZED TECHNOLOGY, COMBINED WITH A
KNOWLEDGE OF THE SEA AND RESPECT FOR ITS LIFE, HAVE ALLOWED COASTAL
PEOPLES TO HARVEST THE SEA'S BOUNTY FOR CENTURIES, WHILE DAMAGING IT
NOT IN THE SLIGHTEST. OFTEN THEIR FISHING METHODS ARE SELECTIVE, SO
THAT THE MINIMUM NUMBER OF FISH ARE TAKEN – IN SHARP CONTRAST TO THE
SWEEP NETS AND HUGE TRAWLERS USED BY THE COMMERCIAL FISHING
INDUSTRY, WHICH 'VACUUM' ALL THE LIFE FROM WHATEVER STRETCH OF SEA
THEY TARGET.

200

201

202   FISHING CANOES OFF THE EAST COAST OF SRI LANKA
(Starfoto/Zefa)
MANY COASTAL PEOPLES ARE EXTREMELY ACCOMPLISHED BOAT-BUILDERS AND
NAVIGATORS, DESPITE HAVING NO INDUSTRIAL TECHNOLOGY, AND MANY STILL
USE TRADITIONAL CRAFT MADE SOLELY FROM NATURAL MATERIALS. FOR PEOPLE
WHO SUBSIST FROM THE SEA, A FISHING BOAT IS A FAMILY'S MOST ESSENTIAL
POSSESSION.

203

204

203 FISHING BOATS AT ERQUY, BRITTANY, FRANCE

(B. & C. Alexander)

EVEN IN EUROPE THERE ARE STILL TRADITIONAL FISHING COMMUNITIES WHOSE SMALL-SCALE OPERATIONS PROVIDE A LIVELIHOOD FOR THE VILLAGE YET ARE SUSTAINABLE WITHOUT HARMING THE ENVIRONMENT. HERE, FISHERMEN APPROACH THE HARBOUR AFTER A DAY'S FISHING. KEEPING BOTH BOATS AND NETS IN GOOD REPAIR IS A HABITUAL TASK.

204 COD-FISHING, NEWFOUNDLAND

(B. & C. Alexander)

EACH SUMMER, THE SMALL CAPELIN FISH HURL THEMSELVES ON TO THE GRAVEL SHORE TO SPAWN, WHEREUPON THEY ARE PURSUED BY SCHOOLS OF COD. THESE FISHERMEN LAY OUT THEIR NETS CLOSE TO THE SHORELINE, IN SUCH A WAY THAT THE COD ARE CHANNELLED INTO A LARGE NET BOX, WHICH THEY EMPTY DAILY. HERE THE CREW ARE HAULING IN THE COD TRAP. SUCH SMALL-SCALE FISHING IS UNLIKELY TO AFFECT COD STOCKS, BUT FISH FACTORY VESSELS HAVE GREATLY DEPLETED THE POPULATIONS OF THIS COMMERCIALLY IMPORTANT FISH – POSSIBLY PERMANENTLY.

205

205 ISLANDERS PREPARE TO DISEMBARK, SATAWAL, MICRONESIA

(B. & C. Alexander)

ISOLATED FROM THE REST OF THE YAP ISLANDS, SATAWAL IS DEPENDENT
ON THIS CARGO AND PASSENGER BOAT TO BRING SUPPLIES AND A DOCTOR
EVERY FEW MONTHS, AND TO TRANSPORT LOCAL PRODUCTS FOR SALE
ELSEWHERE.

206 A FLOATING FISH STALL, THAILAND

(Robert Harding Picture Library)

FLOATING MARKET STALLS SELLING FISH AND OTHER PRODUCE ARE A
COMMON SIGHT AROUND THAILAND'S MANY SMALL ISLANDS. BOTH MARINE
AND FRESHWATER FISHING ARE IMPORTANT TO THE THAI ECONOMY.
MACKEREL, SHARK, SHRIMPS AND CRABS ARE EXPORTED, AND FISH STILL
PROVIDES MOST OF THE PROTEIN IN THE PEOPLE'S DIET. BUT THE SHALLOW
COASTAL WATERS OF THE GULF OF THAILAND ARE BEING GROSSLY OVER-
FISHED BY COMMERCIAL INTERESTS.

216

209

207 and 208   AN INUK WITH HIS DOG TEAM (B. & C. Alexander), **AND AN INUK JIGGING FOR POLAR COD** (B. & C. Alexander), **CANADA**
ONCE THE SEA HAS FROZEN OVER AT THE BEGINNING OF THE WINTER, THE INUIT FIND THEIR HUNTING GROUNDS GREATLY EXTENDED. POLAR BEAR HUNTS, INVOLVING JOURNEYS OVER SEA ICE, USING SLEDS DRAWN BY DOG TEAMS, CAN LAST FOR FOUR TO SIX WEEKS. IN SPRING THE SEA ICE BEGINS TO MELT, AND HUNTING ON IT BECOMES DANGEROUS. FISHING THROUGH HOLES IN THE ICE IS AN EASY, IF TEDIOUS, ALTERNATIVE. ONCE CAUGHT, THE FISH WILL FREEZE ALMOST INSTANTLY IN THE AIR – WHEN THIS PHOTOGRAPH (208) WAS TAKEN THE TEMPERATURE WAS −35° CENTIGRADE.

210

209 and 210   AN INUK PREPARING A SEAL NET (B. & C. Alexander), **AND AN IGLOO AT NIGHT** (B. & C. Alexander), **NORTHWEST GREENLAND**
BEFORE THE SEA FULLY FREEZES IN OCTOBER, THE INUIT TRAVEL TO PLACES WHERE THE SEALS ARE MANY. NETS ARE STRUNG OUT BETWEEN TWO HOLES IN THE ICE BELOW THE SURFACE, AND WEIGHTED DOWN WITH STONES WHERE THE CURRENT IS STRONG; SEALS ARE SWEPT INTO THE CURTAIN OF NET AND HAULED UP. ON LONG HUNTING TRIPS SOME INUIT STILL BUILD THE SHELTERS THAT WE KNOW AS IGLOOS; ONE PERSON CAN CONSTRUCT AN IGLOO IN ABOUT AN HOUR. INUIT HAVE NEVER USED THEM AS PERMANENT HOMES.

CONCLUSION

ROGER HAMMOND

ROCKS MIRROR THE RAVAGES OF WEATHER OVER CENTURIES, AND PEOPLE'S faces hold a lifetime's experience. The sea does not record the passage of time on its endlessly shifting surface: it is almost impossible to comprehend that over three and a half thousand million years have passed since the oceans spawned the first, primitive living organisms.

Evolution works on a giant time scale which defies the imagination. Consider, for example, that small, hooved, dog-like creatures inhabiting prehistoric beaches were the ancestors of today's great whales. The extraordinary metamorphosis took place as generation after generation was selected and refined over some fifty million years. This enormous length of time is nonetheless just a moment in the history of the oceans, and in the history of life itself.

In evolutionary terms, human beings appeared on the scene very recently indeed. They quickly developed a relationship with the sea; communities were living and fishing along the oceans' margins well before 25,000 BC, and by 3,000 BC many were accomplished seafarers. People have exploited the oceans for transport, food and other resources ever since. But until just two or three hundred years ago, we had little impact on the ecosystem: the sea retained ultimate control. Storms wrecked thousand upon thousand of vessels, taking crews and cargo to the ocean bed. Their remains were rapidly assimilated, and the sea's ancient life processes continued, undisturbed.

We are probably little different from our ancestors, but the world we inhabit is dramatically changed. In less than a century, the global population has exploded from 1,700 million to nearly 5,000 million. And thanks to the Industrial Revolution, we have at our disposal powers that our forebears could not have dreamed of. Such conditions have brought unprecedented pressures to bear on the oceans – this most vital of the planet's life support systems.

In the briefest moment of evolutionary time, we have reversed our relationship with the sea: today, we are the ones in control. It is a power we greatly abuse. We are decimating fish stocks and endangering other creatures with indiscriminate fishing methods. Miles of drift-nets spare none; huge factory ships remove hundreds of tonnes of marine life in a single catch. But perhaps even more destructive than this constant depleting is what we pour into the sea. Toxic materials from factories, power stations, ocean tankers, sewage plants and agricultural land are discharged or deliberately dumped into the water. Animals are poisoned and entire species threatened by these alien substances. The thinning ozone layer may present an even graver long-term danger, for it appears to be affecting the growth of phytoplankton – the base of the entire marine ecosystem.

There is one power that we have greatly under-used. We possess at least some understanding of the oceans' global importance, and also of our own impact on them. To date, we have concentrated solely on developing new ways of exploiting more of the sea's resources. We must now begin to channel our abilities differently, and discover how we may balance our needs with what the oceans can provide. The changed world demands a change in attitudes and practices: we must respond to this challenge, if we are to safeguard both our own future, and the oceans'.

A NORTH SEA OIL RIG IN ROUGH WEATHER

(Arnulf Husmo/Tony Stone Worldwide)

ONLY IN THE LAST TWO HUNDRED AND FIFTY YEARS OR SO HAVE HUMAN BEINGS BEEN ABLE TO HARNESS THE SEA'S POWER AND MINERAL RESOURCES, BUT IN THAT TIME WE HAVE DONE IMMEASURABLE DAMAGE TO THE MARINE ECOSYSTEM. CAN WE NOW LEARN TO USE THE OCEANS IN A LESS DESTRUCTIVE WAY?

THE LIVING EARTH FOUNDATION

LIVING EARTH IS ONE OF A NUMBER OF ORGANIZATIONS working internationally to help bring about change. The human being has the unique quality of being able to look forward in time. Our governments must learn to be responsible for the future, just as individuals must learn to be responsible to future generations.

As individuals, at a national level, use your voting and lobbying rights to ensure that politicians develop new regional and international agreements to protect marine ecosystems. At a regional level, ensure that marine parks and protected coastlands are established. By exercising your discretion as a consumer, exert a direct impact on corporations that exploit the oceans. As we approach the end of the twentieth century, it is up to us all to ensure that we can celebrate the oceans' next millennium as well as the present one.

By buying this book you are helping to fund our work along coastal areas in Cameroon, Brazil and Venezuela. Fragile ecosystems in these countries are increasingly under threat of over-exploitation, but by involving local people in conservation and management, Living Earth is turning the tide. Its environmental education programmes are empowering local communities to understand and value their natural heritage and initiate changes in the way they use natural resources.

If you wish to know more about the work of Living Earth, further information can be obtained from our UK office.

Living Earth Foundation,
The Old Laundry, Ossington Buildings,
Moxon Street, London W1M 3JD

CONTRIBUTORS

PROFESSOR DAVID BELLAMY, botanist, writer and broadcaster, is co-founder of the Conservation Foundation and Vice-President of the Marine Conservation Society.

DR JULIAN CALDECOTT is an ecologist. As Biodiversity Management Adviser to the Indonesian government, he has worked on policy issues concerning many large coastal and marine reserves.

DR TUNDI AGARDY is Marine Conservation Scientist for the World Wildlife Fund in the USA.

DR IAN JOINT is a Project Leader at the Plymouth Marine Laboratory of the Natural Environment Research Council, and has worked on various aspects of phytoplankton ecology for the past twenty years.

MARK SIMMONDS is a campaigning marine biologist and Senior Lecturer in Environmental Sciences at the University of Greenwich in London. He has worked closely for several years with Greenpeace, focusing on the impacts of pollution on marine wildlife.

DR MARTIN ANGEL is head of the Biology Department at the Institute of Oceanographic Sciences, Deacon Laboratory, Surrey. In addition to his chapter, he has provided a great deal of expertise and support in the preparation of this book.

DR PETER HERRING is Senior Scientist in the Biology Department of the Institute of Oceanographic Sciences, Deacon Laboratory, Surrey.

DR ANDREW WATSON is Senior Scientist at the Plymouth Marine Laboratory.

SIR ANTHONY LAUGHTON is a marine geophysicist who has researched into the nature and origin of the geology of the ocean basins. His special interest is the shape and structure of the ocean floor. He is the former Director of the Institute of Oceanographic Sciences, Surrey, and a past President of the Challenger Society for Marine Science.

DR NICHOLAS POLUNIN is a Lecturer in the Department of Marine Sciences and Coastal Management at the University of Newcastle.

PROFESSOR ALASTAIR COUPER teaches in the Department of Maritime Studies, University of Wales, Cardiff, and is the former Editor of the *Times Atlas of the Oceans*.

ROGER HAMMOND is the Founder Director and Chief Executive of Living Earth.

LISA SILCOCK is a freelance writer, photographer and film-maker with a special interest in environmental issues. She was assistant producer of Channel 4's award-winning series, *Baka – People of the Rainforest*. She edited the previous book in this series, *The Rainforests: A Celebration*, and has contributed to numerous national publications.

HELEN GILKS, who researched the illustrations for this book, manages the international Wildlife Photographer of the Year Competition.

DAMIEN LEWIS is an award-winning journalist and film-maker, who specializes in environment and development issues.

ROBERT BISSET is a Director of the World Press Centre, and the co-ordinator of their Oceans Service.

ACKNOWLEDGEMENTS

The publishers would like to thank the following individuals and agencies for permission to use their photographs in this book:

BRYAN & CHERRY ALEXANDER
Higher Cottage
Manston
Sturminster Newton
Dorset DT10 1EZ
UK
tel 0258 473006

HEATHER ANGEL/BIOFOTOS
Highways
6 Vicarage Hill
Farnham
Surrey GU9 8HJ
UK
tel 0252 716700

LAURIE CAMPBELL
Rosewell Cottage
Paxton
Berwick-upon-Tweed TD15 1TE
tel 0289 86736

GERRY ELLIS NATURE
PHOTOGRAPHY
6208 South West 32nd Avenue
Portland
Oregon 97201
USA
fax 503 452 1914

DAVID HALL
257 Ohayo Mountain Road
Woodstock
New York 12498
USA
fax 914 334 4788

ROBERT HARDING PICTURE
LIBRARY
58-59 Great Marlborough Street
London W1V 1DD
tel 071 287 5414

RICHARD HERRMANN
12545 Mustang Drive
Poway
CA 92064
USA
tel 619 679 7017

INSTITUTE OF OCEANOGRAPHIC
SCIENCES (IOS)
Wormley
Godalming
Surrey GU9 5UB
UK
tel 0428 684141

BURT JONES & MAURINE
SHIMLOCK
Secret Sea Visions
PO Box 162931
Austin
Tex. 78716
USA
tel/fax 512 328 1201

J. MICHAEL KELLY
102 East Moore
Suite 245
Terrell
Tex. 75160
USA
fax 214 563 2515

ARMIN MAYWALD
Graf Moltke Strasse 59
2800 Bremen 1
Germany
tel 0421 358 907

MINDEN PICTURES
24 Seascape Village
Aptos
CA 95003
USA
fax 408 685 1911

DAVID NOTON
20 Doone Road
Horfield
Bristol BS7 0JG
UK
tel 0272 512489

BEN OSBORNE
c/o Oxford Scientific Films
Lower Road
Long Hanborough
Oxfordshire OX8 8LL
UK
tel 0993 881881

OXFORD SCIENTIFIC FILMS
(OSF)
Lower Road
Long Hanborough
Oxfordshire OX8 8LL
UK
tel 0993 881881

LINDA PITKIN
12 Coningsby Road
South Croydon
Surrey CR2 6QP
UK

PLANET EARTH PICTURES
4 Harcourt Street
London W1H 1DS
tel 071 262 4427

GRAHAM ROBERTSON
c/o Australian Antarctic Division
Channel Highway
Kingston
Tasmania 7050
Australia

JEFF ROTMAN PHOTOGRAPHY
14 Cottage Avenue
Somerville
MA 02144
USA
fax 617 666 4811

TONY STONE WORLDWIDE
Worldwide House
116 Bayham Street
London NW1 0BA
tel 071 267 7166

KIM WESTERSKOV
20 Greerton Road
Tauranga
New Zealand
tel 75 785 138

NORBERT WU
165 Ivy Drive
Orinda
CA 94563
USA
fax 510 376 8864

ZEFA PICTURE LIBRARY
20 Conduit Place
London W2 1HZ
tel 071 262 0101